DATE			

BAKER & TAYLOR

THE TEAM-BASED
PROBLEM SOLVER

THE TEAM-BASED PROBLEM SOLVER

Joan P. Klubnik

Penny F. Greenwood

IRWIN
Professional Publishing
Burr Ridge, Illinois
New York, New York

Senior sponsoring editor: Cynthia A. Zigmund
Project editor: Lynne Basler
Production manager: Laurie Kersch
Interior designer: Mercedes Santos
Cover designer: Tim Kaage
Art manager: Heather Burbridge
Compositor: TCSystems, Inc.
Typeface: 11/13 Palatino
Printer: Book Press, Inc.

Library of Congress Cataloging-in-Publication Data

Klubnik, Joan P.
    The team-based problem solver / Joan P. Klubnik and Penny F. Greenwood.
      p.   cm.
    Includes bibliographical references and index.
    ISBN 0-7863-0187-2
    1. Work groups. 2. Group problem solving. I. Greenwood, Penny
F. II. Title.
HD66.K59 1995 .
658.4'036—dc20   94–1191

The Team-Based Problem Solver *is dedicated to the memory of David Bradford, Beta Site Engineer, Total Quality Supplier Development Program, SEMATECH.*

David's commitment to ensuring that the concepts and tools of Total Quality learned in the classroom would be transferred to the workplace was an impetus to the completion of this guidebook. His active support of the project and thorough critique of the early drafts was invaluable. May his memory serve as a guide to all of us who struggle with making the process work.

We wish to thank all who have offered their suggestions in the development of this guidebook. We are especially grateful to the trainers, team leaders, and group participants of our client groups who actively assessed its application to their unique work situations and took the time to give us honest, useful feedback. And to our families who put up with us throughout the process.

The guidebook is the product of continuous revising and reworking. We welcome all suggestions you may have for making this book more useful to you in your quality improvement efforts.

Preface

Who Will Benefit from **The Team-Based Problem Solver?**

This book is for you: the employee, public official, volunteer, or student who recognizes that your own competitive advantage, as well as your organization's, will come from your being a skilled team player and problem solver.

Who on the Team Needs a Copy of **The Team-Based Problem Solver?**

To do team-based problem solving, team effort is explicitly required. By definition then, it is a group activity. This means that you and your team will be involved in *working sessions* as you move through the steps that lead to your resolving your problem. These can almost be equated to conducting a series of workshops. For this reason the book is designed to be the workbook that each team member uses as his or her guide throughout the process.

The book is your reference for the steps to follow in solving a team-based problem. It can help you to apply the specific tools and techniques you need at any given point in the process. The overall process is shown at the beginning of each chapter with the current step highlighted.

Why a Disk for the Forms?

The disk provides a source for blank copies of all the forms discussed in the book. The intent is that you assimilate the model (either in detail or abbreviated) and use the forms needed to address any problem you are currently facing. You will find that some problems, because of their complexity, will result in your using many of the forms and tools; other problems will only require a few as aids and memory joggers. Because the forms are on disk, you can easily produce those you need in any quantity. By copying a form into a new file, you can also modify that form to meet your particular needs, whether it be space or title related.

Why Include a Scenario?

The scenario allows you to walk through the team-based problem solver process by seeing how it applies to an actual problem a team is addressing. As the Scenario team works through their problem, they use a number of the tools that are introduced in the main text and detailed in the Appendixes.

A group often approaches a problem thinking that it can be solved in one or two sessions. Our scenario is quite long to show you a multitude of tools, it is important to recognize that effective problem solving generally takes time. A careful analysis of the actual problem often results in a more time-consuming resolution process. This is usually driven by a need to get more information (from customers as well as from peers), to gather hard data to support what the team is identifying by gut and experience, and to validate the process that is recommended. Be wary of problem-resolution processes that are always quick—you may well be overlooking or short changing important elements that are the basis of honest resolution of root problems.

How to Use the Appendixes?

The appendixes have been designed to provide you with background information and exhibits of the forms to support your application of the problem-solving tools and techniques. Throughout the book itself and in the scenario, forms and techniques included in the appendixes are referenced. We encourage you to use this support material as much as you need. If you have not been exposed to problem-solving tools in the past, the information in the appendixes will walk you through their use. We have divided the materials as follows:

APPENDIX A: PROBLEM-SOLVING TOOLS TO HELP YOU EXPAND YOUR RANGE OF IDEAS	Includes tools you might consider using when you are trying to expand your view of the problem or of alternatives available to you at a given point in the resolution process.
APPENDIX B: ANALYSIS TOOLS TO HELP YOU GAIN FOCUS ON SOLUTIONS	Includes tools to help you reduce the scope of the alternatives you are considering. It will help you cull through ideas to determine which are the most viable alternatives to consider further.
APPENDIX C: PLANNING AND MONITORING TOOLS	Includes tools that will help you track your progress through the problem-solving process.
APPENDIX D: TIPS AND TECHNIQUES FOR BUILDING A TEAM	The heart of the problem-solving process is the team itself. This appendix contains information to help you build and enhance your group's ability to work as a team.
APPENDIX E: PREPARING YOUR PRESENTATION: PRESENTATION TIPS	The problem-solving team must be prepared to "sell" their ideas to key process players. This appendix contains helpful tips to assist the team in preparing the best possible presentation.
APPENDIX F: LEARNING TRANSFERENCE WORKSHEET	A worksheet to use after your problem-solving initiative has been completed.

Advantage Leadership
Joan P. Klubnik
Penny F. Greenwood

Contents

Setting the Scene
Why Use a Team-Based Approach

GOAL: To provide an overview of the team-based problem solving model and to provide the rationale for why today's work teams should apply such a process to their problems.

Why Team-Based Problem Solving?
What Is Team-Based Problem Solving?
Why a Systematic Problem-Solving Process?
The Problem-Solving Model—Process Overview
The Book Format
Using This Book in Your Team Meetings
Summary

WHY TEAM-BASED PROBLEM SOLVING?

Today's businesses are rapidly moving to smaller and flatter organizations that are using teams and self-directed work groups to carry on day-to-day business. Economic and work-force changes are driving these new approaches to doing business. Whenever we ask a group of our workshop participants what is the value for their company of their attending our workshop, The Team-Based Problem Solver, we hear, "Survival."

Public and private organizations and institutions are recognizing the need for working in teams and using structured processes for problem solving, goal setting, and so forth. However they are finding that the skills and methods needed for this new environment are not as readily available within the work force or easy to construct as hoped for.

Western civilization has focused on the individual. We are held accountable for our individual actions and performance. Socially we may enjoy groups, but in our educational and work environments, we have been encouraged to stand alone. Solving our problems, addressing issues and using our creative power has become our individual shield of identity. Now we are told to work together, so that our outcomes will be better, faster, cheaper. We hear that the sum of the parts is greater than the individual components. That may be, and there is lots of data that supports the quality of team effort, but it still feels wrong, uncomfortable, and time consuming.

Our goal is to help you overcome these feelings, to recognize and value the richness of group interaction, and to appreciate the quality of your work. We will help you learn a process and techniques to assist you in integrating the knowledge, talents, and skills of all your team members into a highly functioning productive team.

WHAT IS TEAM-BASED PROBLEM SOLVING?

Most guides to problem solving focus on learning a structured, problem-solving model. A few discuss the value of working on team dynamics and give suggestions on how to do it, but we have actively integrated at each step of a problem-solving model a corresponding focus on the team dynamics that may influence that step. This book, an outgrowth of our Team-Based Problem Solver workshop, specifically focuses on this integration. To be an effective problem solver, you must develop good team interaction skills. The team-based problem-solving process overlays the stages of group development, a theory first developed by Bruce Tuckman in 1965, and refined over the years by numerous organizational development practitioners, with a systematic problem-solving process.

The model shown in Figure 1–1 recognizes that as a group forms to select and clearly define the issue to be addressed, the first step of the problem-solving process, they are also in the first stage of team development, the *forming stage*. The behaviors evident at this stage—tentativeness, testing the waters, asking if you're the right person to be on the team, etc., have a direct influence on the quality of the information generated and the time it takes to complete the entire problem-solving process.

This guide recognizes the interaction that takes place at each stage and provides a number of tools and techniques to assist you

FIGURE 1–1

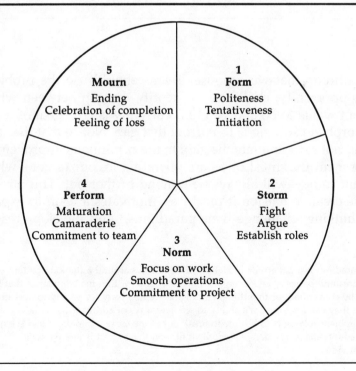

in dealing effectively with the team life-cycle dynamics you may encounter at various points in the problem-solving process. We have identified a number of traps that may occur and have provided suggestions on how to avoid or mitigate them.

An example is shown in the following box:

Trap:	Getting hung up on words. Is it a problem, an issue, an opportunity, or a challenge? Some people prefer to talk about *problems*—everyone has problems, so "tell it as it really is." Others prefer to think in terms of *issues*—they are neutral; and others think of *opportunities*, or *challenges*—these are positive approaches.
Solution:	Don't let semantics get in the way—the entire group must be conscious of this potential trap and be prepared to address it when it surfaces.

An attitude that we espouse: Teams should use the problem, issue, opportunity, challenge to identify the gap between where the team wants to be and where it currently is. The goal of team-based problem solving is to narrow that gap. Notice that the solution did not say eliminate the gap. In the continuous improvement environment that most of us are operating in, our target—where we want to be—will always be moving further out. This stretch, and the creative tension it produces, motivates a team to expand their thinking, challenge their paradigms,* and develop creative

---

* A paradigm is a pattern or model. It provides rules around a thinking pattern or content area and basically tells everyone how to operate within the boundaries that have been set by convention for that thing. Paradigms are necessary for society to operate; however, they can limit a team's ability to see new ways of addressing a situation. A goal of problem solving is to be able to break out of the current paradigm and see new ways of addressing a situation. An excellent film on this subject is Joel Barker's paradigm video.

solutions that will serve as the foundation for the next solution stretch.

WHY A SYSTEMATIC
PROBLEM-SOLVING PROCESS?

The majority of problems we encounter in today's society are increasing in complexity at the same time that less time and resources are available to solve them. Our mode of operandi has been to institute short fixes, treating numerous symptoms but not the actual root causes of the problem. However we are beginning to recognize that the time and money dedicated to rework, retooling, false starts, and so on, are draining our resources and greatly impacting our competitive edge. Business is beginning to recognize that dedicating resources up front by instituting structured group problem solving will result in reduced cost and error, maximized results, improved communication among departments and employees, and increased personal satisfaction for our work force.

A systematic, team-based problem-solving process is a disciplined approach for achieving these benefits, and it provides the tools and techniques necessary to overcome the barriers that you'll encounter. This is a change process, and whenever change is instituted, you need to be prepared to deal with resistance, fear, sacred cows, and old habits. By using the problem-solving model provided, you and your team members will develop the skills and knowledge necessary to collect and use data effectively, be creative, manage conflict, clearly define your issue, select the best solution from among many, plan your implementation and monitor results. The model will provide you with a map for navigating through typical traps that can prevent quality solutions.

The problem-solving model is shown in two formats—short and detailed.

A more detailed model breaking out the processes involved in each step and the goal for that step is shown on the next page. You can use this more detailed model as a quick refresher guide for the process after you have worked through it and are comfortable with the process steps and tools.

FIGURE 1–2
The Problem-Solving Model

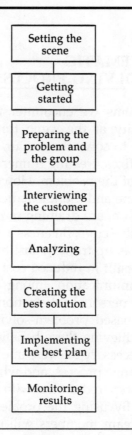

THE PROBLEM-SOLVING MODEL— PROCESS OVERVIEW

Step One: Getting Started—Establishing and Maintaining Your Process Road Map

Goal. Develop a framework for team interaction so that the problem-solving model can be used successfully.

- Establish your meeting format—how do we want to work?
- Team organization—how will we be managed?

- Team interaction guidelines—what are our guiding principles?
- Process check—how will we monitor our progress?

Step Two: Preparing the Problem and the Group

Goal. Clarify the issue and gain agreement on the problem to be addressed.

- Surface the problem
- Define the problem
- Develop the problem statement
- Assess readiness to move forward

Step Three: Interviewing Customers

Goal. Determine who your external and internal customers are and what they expect from the process you are working on.

- Identify the customers who will be affected
- Develop interview questions
- Interview customers
- Quantify customer concerns
- Refine the problem statement

Step Four: Analyzing Causes

Goal. Thoroughly analyze all causes of the problem before beginning problem resolution.

- Cause identification and analysis—individual
- Cause identification—group
- Understand all the causes
- Determine the root cause(s)—rank the causes
- Collect and analyze data on root causes

Step Five: Creating the Best Solution

Goal. Generate and critique all potential actions *before* committing to a plan. Design and implement a plan to solve the problem.

- Generate promising solutions
- Select the best solution(s)
- Develop an implementation plan
- Develop measures to monitor performance

Step Six: Implementing the Plan

Goal. Obtain commitment from key parties for actions that have been clearly defined.

- Gain organizational/personal commitment
- Plan for marketing your solution
- Execute the plan and prepare for the future

Step Seven: Monitoring Results

Goal. Your problem solution solves the problem and leads to customer satisfaction and continuous improvement.

- Plan for a postmortem
- Plan for follow-up
- Plan for continuous improvement
- Future think
- Final process check
- Communicate results
- Saying thank you
- Congratulations!

THE BOOK FORMAT

The first section of the book is devoted to understanding and preparing for team-based problem solving. It includes this introduction and Getting Started: The Process Road Map. This is followed by a detailed description of each of the remaining steps in the team-based problem-solving process. Complementing this step-by-step description is a scenario that incorporates the tools and techniques into an actual team setting. The scenario highlights the dynamic challenges and opportunities that might occur at each stage in the process. The scenario segments occur at the end of each chapter. The last section of the book is the Appendixes. Here you will find the tools grouped by type, presentation tips, process tips, and so forth.

USING THIS BOOK IN YOUR TEAM MEETINGS

The first thing to do is review the Process Road Map introduced in the next section, Getting Started. This section provides a starting point for team formation and outlines the mechanics for each team session. Once you've completed your upfront planning, you're ready to begin addressing the problem. Each chapter will walk you through a step and suggest appropriate tools to use at that point in the process. All the tools are listed in the Appendixes.

Be sure to note the traps identified at different points in the process. Spending some time ensuring that you are not heading for a trap can save overall time in problem resolution even though it may seem that the process is taking too much time initially. (Pay me now; pay me later.) Recognize that you may need to have several meetings in order to complete a step. The time dedicated to each step will depend on how long you can meet, the type of problem you are addressing, the amount and type of data you'll need to collect, the team dynamics you're experiencing, and so forth.

It is imperative to realize that you won't successfully move forward until unresolved team issues are surfaced and addressed. You must plan for, and allow time for, dealing with inter-personal issues. Using the process checks will assist you in objectively raising and dealing with outstanding issues. Once they are dealt with, your team has the potential to arrive at an outstanding solution.

SUMMARY

Team problem solving requires that the team meet to expand ideas, focus thinking, deal with issues, and get the work done. Today's organization is putting the focus on teamwork and putting resources into developing teams because the end produces greater quality results. The successes already achieved in customer satisfaction, quality processes, and employee empowerment are proving that effective teams do make a difference. Our objective is to help you increase your personal competitive advantage by quickly becoming an effective team player and problem solver. Using this guide will assist you and your team to more quickly achieve a quality solution, to add value to the organization that you are supporting and to enhance its competitive edge.

SCENARIO

INTRODUCTION

Mary and Jan opened a small restaurant in a downtown office complex four years ago. They have been quite successful, specializing in breakfast and lunch. They have counter service, a sit-down restaurant that seats 32, and a fairly sizable takeout business. In the last year, they expanded into catering office meetings and company parties. This was a big step. The upfront investment was significant, requiring a new bank loan plus home-equity money from both of them. Although the marketing forecast is healthy for this expansion, they are very concerned that it be a financial success. A great deal of time is being spent on growing this business segment. The forecast of income for each business segment for the current year is:

Restaurant	55%
Counter	5%
Takeout	30%
Catering	10%

Until the last six weeks, actual versus forecast was fairly accurate. In fact Catering is coming on so strong that Jan thinks it may contribute close to 15 percent of total revenue by year's end. However, Takeout has taken a sudden shift downwards. Mary and Jan are quite concerned. They have always been able to count on the stability of their Takeout business.

Mary had recently attended a small business seminar that focused on the value of work force empowerment. She realized that she and Jan may not have taken full advantage of their staff's skills and knowledge. Being in a start-up situation for so long, she and Jan had fallen into the trap of doing things themselves, forgetting that as they added staff, they could have drawn them into their planning and problem-solving activities. Mary purchased a copy of the *Team-Based Problem Solver* and began to consider how she could use it at the restaurant. (*To be continued on page 35.*)

Getting Started—
Establishing and Maintaining Your Process Road Map

GOAL: *Develop a framework for team interaction so that the problem-solving model can be used successfully.*

.Getting started	Preparing the problem and the group	Interviewing the customer	Analyzing	Creating the best solution	Implementing the best plan	Monitoring results

Establish Your Meeting Format—How Do We Want to Work?

Team Organization—How Will We Be Managed?

Team Interaction Guidelines—What Are Our Guiding Principles?

Process Check—How Will We Monitor Our Progress?

The team is responsible for ensuring that the road map is followed. This section focuses on those process elements that have been identified as being critical for effective team performance. This refers to both the way team members interact with each other during problem-solving sessions and also how well the team follows and completes each step of the model.

Trap:	You have never worked in a team environment before to solve a problem and you don't know what it should look like, so you short cut the steps because you are uncomfortable with trying something new.
Solution:	Consider having an outside facilitator come in to help your team understand and practice using the process, tools and techniques that the team isn't comfortable with.

The reason for following the road map is to establish an environment where team members are open with each other—this is based on respect and trust. Such groups are more successful in their problem-solving activities because they are better able to manage the people process. It is quite natural for differences to surface between team members as the problem-solving process proceeds. In fact an indicator of a group's potential is the amount of conflict they encounter early in the process. The more conflict the better potential for an exceptional solution. Such a group is probably generating a lot of ideas and exhibiting energy and commitment, elements critical to good team performance. However, if they don't have the skills to manage this early conflict, they usually become a nonperforming team.

Team members need the skills that allow the group to resolve its differences to the satisfaction of all members. This generally requires a willingness for members to respect other's views and to negotiate acceptable resolutions to differences.

This section includes specific process techniques and tools that can help your team work together effectively. These tools are presented before the actual problem-solving process is started because they lay the foundation for the group's being able to work through the process.

ESTABLISH YOUR MEETING FORMAT— HOW DO WE WANT TO WORK?

The heart of problem solving is the working meeting. The success of your team meetings will determine the success you have in solving your problem. Some keys to improve the probability that your meetings are successful:

Establish and follow meeting guidelines. These are the rules your team agrees are important and that they agree to abide by whenever they come together. Since they dictate behavior, it is important that every member agree to the list. Allow time for the team to reach consensus around what should be included. (See Appendix B, Page 191 for a definition of consensus.)

Once you have determined your guidelines, record them on the Guideline in Appendix C, page 193. If you keep the list visible— posted or as a handout—it will be easier for the group to live by its own rules of conduct. The items listed below are guidelines specifically focused on meeting management and are ones that many teams have adopted. Consider, but don't blindly adopt, the list—select management guides that meet the needs of your team. The key is to take the time to create a list, post it, review it periodically, and enforce what you, as a group, say is important for meetings to be successful:

Potential meeting management guidelines

- People must be on time—start all sessions on time.
- The agenda is to be followed—published ahead of time and reviewed at the beginning of each session.
- Ensure proper facilities and equipment.
- Predetermine if the meeting needs a facilitator and/or a scribe (note taker).
- Key people must be present for the meeting to be held.
- Remember the 3 C's—consensus, courtesy, confidentiality.
- Regularly ask: Is this meeting necessary?
- Follow the team guidelines you establish to manage the interpersonal dynamics of your sessions.
- Requisite materials must be available at the meeting.

> **Problem solving can be a very complex and involved process so it is important to review—to make sure that all members are together in their thinking and ready to address the problem.**

Establish and follow agendas.   No meeting should be held without a preestablished agenda. Depending on the informality of the group, it may not have to be typed up and distributed, but no one should ever call a meeting without preplanning. A basic agenda format is shown below. The last portion of the agenda addresses how you intend to evaluate the meetings you just held and what steps need to occur outside of the current meeting to prepare for the next one. These follow-through items are often forgotten, yet they are critical to continuous improvement of both the meetings themselves and team process.

> **Consider keeping your agendas and minutes as a historical record of your team problem solving. If you maintain a central repository of agendas with associated problem-solving data, completed forms and tools, others in your organization can frequently learn from the experiences of one team and thus shorten time frames and improve the quality of similar future problem-solving efforts.**

Consider the basic mechanics below to help your sessions flow smoothly:

1. *Where* and *when* will you meet, and *who* will be responsible for making sure that meeting space is reserved for your group? These might seem like simple tasks, and they are, but they are critical to the teams that meet regularly. Most business complexes today have limited space that is at a premium—meetings must be planned ahead and room reservations made. Also, be sure that the facility you plan to use has the proper equipment (flip charts, overheads, computers for documentation purposes, etc.).

2. *How long* will each session last? Most teams find that a one-and-a-half to two-hour session is productive. One key to such a time limit is that you **start on time**—everyone must agree to be at the site and ready to start at the appointed time. Another key is

Meeting Agenda (Appendex C, Page 194)

Team: _____   Date: _____
                              Time—start: _____ end: _____
                              Location: _____
Leader: _____   Timekeeper: _____
Facilitator: _____ Scribe: _____
Purpose:

Meeting preparation: Background/Premeeting assignments:

                          Please bring:

Agenda Item	Responsible Person	Process to Address Topic	Time	Expected Outcome	Actual Outcome*

End-of-meeting planning: Evaluation technique/process: _____
                           Action to be taken: _____

*To be filled at the next meeting to be sure that there are no unfinished items and to document actions agreed to.

that everyone comes prepared. (Decide how to deal with nonconformity up front before it becomes an issue.)

3. Identify any *time limits* the team wants set on discussions. Most of your sessions will be driven by some sort of agenda (even if it is informal). As a part of the agenda-setting process, be sure to decide up front how long you will permit a specific discussion to last. When you get close to the limit, query the team:

- Do they want closure at this point?
- Do they want to continue the discussion further?
- Do they want to table the issue to a future meeting?
- Do they want to assign individuals to work on the topic outside of the group meeting and bring information back?

Any of these alternatives is appropriate as long as the entire group agrees. The value of setting a time limit is that it lets the team consciously decide where it is in a particular discussion. Sometimes teams get caught up in their conversation and lose sight of the original purpose or simply continue a circular conversation that is wasteful of time. A time limit helps to control this process problem. If your discussion will exceed 30 minutes, you might want to allow time for a break.

Meeting mechanics. The following process tips will assure that your meetings begin and end effectively. At the beginning of each meeting:

- Review team guidelines.
- Review agenda and role assignment.
- Adjust agenda and time as necessary.

At the end of each meeting:

- Develop next meeting agenda.
- Assign roles if rotating.
- Save data generated. (note: all data is held until the project is successfully completed.)
- Complete process check.

TEAM ORGANIZATION—HOW WILL WE BE MANAGED?

Usually the initial team membership and the issue the team is to address is assigned by management or by a total quality steering committee. The team may also be assigned a leader and/or a team facilitator. It is then the team's responsibility as it moves into the process to ascertain if the membership is correct and to clearly define its expectations of the role of the leader and/or facilitator. Since these roles are often confused, we define a leader as the person responsible for keeping the focus on the charge assigned to the team. It is the leader's job to ensure that the right content is being addressed. The leader is usually intimately familiar with the issue, thoroughly understands the business need and implications of solving the problem, and/or has a high stake in successfully achieving the desired result.

A team leader must have knowledge of the issue, access to resources, the confidence of management to get things done and keep them informed, the respect of the team, and the leadership skills necessary for keeping the team focused on the issue. Team leaders can be managers, but managers are not automatically team leaders. Position in the company hierarchy does not automatically mean being a team leader. Some managers are too closely involved with the problem to see the big picture or do not have the respect of others who will be involved in the problem-resolution process.

Trap:	Always looking to the highest-ranking person or the one with the best political connections to be the leader, to be the person who takes charge, assigns various roles to other group members, and to predominate in all discussions.
Solution:	If the team decides that having a leader is appropriate, during the first or second meeting answer the questions below and then select a leader based on group responses.

A facilitator is not intimately involved in the issue at hand and does not have a vested interest in the outcome. The facilitator is responsible for assisting the group to work to their full potential. The focus is on providing the framework and the building blocks necessary for a group to move through the steps of problem solving so they successfully meet their charge.

The facilitator encourages open communications, builds effective group dynamics, and uses the team-based problem-solving tools and techniques that help a team keep focused and organized. Some characteristics of individuals who effectively fill this role include:

- Being a good listener.
- Being adept at hearing what is said and then synthesizing and paraphrasing team-member comments.
- Asking discussion-opening questions.
- Smoothing conflict.
- Having the respect of the team, which enables the individual to guide the process.

Trap:	Not realizing the unique set of skills required of a skilled facilitator and assuming that everyone on the team can fill the job at some time in the process.
Solution:	Providing in-depth training for those who have the desire and probable ability to act as team facilitators. It is suggested that an organization seek a training resource for its facilitators—generally an extended program of two or more weeks spread out over time so that skills can be developed and practiced under the guidance of experts.

Because of the special skills required of the facilitator, organizations tend to train a few individuals to serve in this capacity, hire individuals with specific expertise as facilitators, or bring in consultants to assist teams as needed. Any of these approaches make available individuals who can be assigned to teams or requested by a team that believes a trained facilitator might be able to assist them work more effectively.

The models of team leadership that we most often encounter are:

- Assigned leader and facilitator.
- Group-selected leader and an assigned facilitator.
- Group-identified leader and/or facilitator.
- Assigned leader who also functions as the facilitator.

We prefer that a team be given a charge, assigned a sponsor who is available as an interface for them, and then allowed to choose their own leader. A process for clarifying the role of leader is outlined below. Even if a team is assigned a leader and/or facilitator, the group should discuss how those roles will be carried out within the team.

Occasionally the role of leader and facilitator can be combined. More and more of today's current and future leaders recognize the need to be skilled in facilitating change and empowering others. They are actively building their facilitation skill base and endorsing the team approach. A person with both the business and facilitation expertise can occasionally serve in both roles.

Trap:	Assuming that every team must have a leader.
Solution:	Designated leadership may not be appropriate for your problem-solving team. Depending on the problem, the corporate roles of those included on the team, and the politics associated with the issue, it is an option to **not have** someone identified as the team leader. Discuss fully what your options are and whether or not designated leadership is appropriate for your team. To do this, you will need to contact the problem's champion to determine if the team can take ownership of its own process.

If you are going to have a team-designated leader, the first step is for the team to develop guidelines for leadership and to identify what support will be given by the rest of the group. It is best to select the leader by consensus—potential leaders can be identified by volunteering or by nomination.

Clarifying the Team Leader and Facilitator Role

These roles will be unique to each team; therefore, you will need to establish your own profile for the positions. As a way of getting ready to do this, your team will need to think about the three areas described below—each addresses a different attribute of team leadership and facilitation. As part of the discussion, consider topics such as group recourse if leadership fails to meet its commitments and/or the possibility of rotating leadership responsibilities. A complete copy of the worksheet is at the end of the section.

The description of desired behaviors—what does a good team leader look like to your group. Think of the facilitator; how are this person's skills the same and different from those of the leader. This will help you decide if one person can fill both roles for your problem-solving team. The data you collect needs to be behavioral because you are drawing a road map for the actions you want in your leader and facilitator.

The identification of inappropriate behaviors—these are the leadership or quasi-management actions that won't work with your team. This doesn't mean they are wrong, they are just inappropriate for your particular group.

Example: a team of very senior technicians definitely would not want a leader or facilitator who tried to take charge and tell the group how to do their tasks (an authoritarian style).

The identification of team-member support initiatives. What will team members do to support the roles of leader and facilitator. This reinforces the point that everyone is responsible for the success of the team.

TEAM LEADERSHIP—WHAT DOES IT LOOK LIKE FOR US?

In the space provided below, write your responses to the questions. When you are done, discuss your answers with the team. As a group, define the leader and facilitator roles for your team and identify the support responsibilities of the team members. These will then become part of your team guidelines.

1. How do you want these roles performed?
   team leader?   facilitator?

   _____   _____

   _____   _____

   _____   _____

2. What don't you want from your
   leader?   facilitator?

   _____   _____

   _____   _____

   _____   _____

3. How can you effectively support the initiatives and efforts of your team leadership?

   _____

   _____

   _____

Support Roles

In addition to the facilitator and leader roles, some other clearly defined roles within the team assist in keeping the team working effectively. The value of roles is that they:

- Give permission to team members to take responsibility to see that all members abide by the guidelines that the group itself established.
- Depersonalize control.

It is not Susie reminding Mary to let John talk, it is the role of the gatekeeper reminding Mary. This may seem to be a nonexistent or superficial difference, but in actuality, it completely changes the message and thus helps to prevent Mary from taking personally what can be interpreted as a rebuke from Susie.

Specific Team Roles

Four key roles are described below. Although they are spelled out separately, one person can wear many of the hats simultaneously. If your team has not paid a great deal of attention to process in the past, you may want to intentionally divide up the roles until people become familiar and comfortable with each hat.

Scribe. It is the responsibility of this person to capture the content of the session. The scribing might be done via flip charts that later can be transcribed. It might mean taking detailed notes or minutes to be distributed to the group after the session. In today's high-tech world, it is quite common for a scribe to use a computer to record what is said with the information simultaneously being shown on a screen so the entire group can see the data as it is captured. In some situations, it is appropriate to have someone record key ideas on flip charts that everyone can see and use as memory joggers; and at the same time, having another person taking detailed notes that are shared after transcribing.

Gatekeeper.* It is the responsibility of this role to monitor the team's process and dynamics. Sometimes when a team focuses

---

*Think of gatekeeping in terms of function, not person. The responsibility can fall to: a separate person (inside or outside the team), the facilitator, or to the leader.

intently on a topic, they forget to consider *how* they are interacting with each other. The gatekeeper has to pull back from the content of the session—instead, he or she focuses on how the group interacts.

This role requires someone who is somewhat removed from the topic and who is able to address another person's behavior in a positive way. Some of the tasks of the gatekeeper include:

- Making sure that members listen to each other.
- Seeing that everyone participates.
- Adhering to the guidelines that the group developed for itself.
- Being sure that comments focus on issues, not on individuals or personalities.

Trap:	Thinking that it is only the official gatekeeper who has responsibility for group process.
Solution:	By whatever means necessary (training, team building, group discussion) assuring that each person within the team assumes responsibility for effective group process. This requires accepting the input from the gatekeeper and owning one's own behavior.

Timekeeper. It is the responsibility of this role to help the team keep track of time during meetings and working sessions and to see that the group adheres to its agreed-upon time schedule.

This does not mean that the team cannot change its direction if all members agree, it simply means that decisions concerning time must be made consciously. The timekeeper helps the team keep to the original time plan. This person takes responsibility for warning the group when its allotted time is almost up—the team can then decide how to proceed.

Contact. It is the responsibility of this person to act as the team liaison. If the problem-solving process is ongoing or lengthy, it may be necessary to report on progress at specific checkpoints. This may also be true if the team has many stakeholders (individuals with a vested interest in the outcome of the problem-solving session) who need to be kept abreast of progress. The contact acts as the *representative* (not leader) of the team to see that necessary information is relayed to others. Even if the entire team participates in the presentation of information, it is helpful to have an identified contact person.

TEAM INTERACTION GUIDELINES—WHAT ARE OUR GUIDING PRINCIPLES?

Team guidelines keep the problem-solving process on track by providing techniques for dealing with group process—how individuals work together. Guidelines help your team prevent or deal with ineffective interpersonal dynamics as they arise. They help you depersonalize how you deal with behaviors that fall outside agreed-to group norms. The guidelines you establish will simplify your working together. When handled appropriately, they help your group focus on the problem at hand; when ignored, they can become a hindrance to the problem-solving process. *Practice effective interpersonal skills*—team members must be able to interact effectively. Check your team—how good are they in dealing with each other?

1. Have you had any team building to help the group learn to appreciate each other's strengths and contributions to the team?
2. Have you had any conflict resolution/negotiations training?
3. Do you have any difficult people on the team? If so, how does the group deal with different traits?
4. Have you participated in any communications training designed to teach the group how to: listen actively, paraphrase, use "I" language?
5. How assertive (not aggressive or passive) are team members?

The questions focus on the interpersonal skill level of group members. The more positive responses, the more likely your group will be able to deal with the dynamics that can interfere with the group's effectiveness.

> If most of your answers are negative, consider some group dynamics training before you proceed with your problem solving. This is especially true if you are dealing with difficult, complex, or sensitive issues.

Agree-on behavioral guidelines. Behavioral guidelines help your team to monitor its group dynamics to assure that all team members are able to participate freely and that they feel their contributions are meaningful to the group's progress.

Behaviors That Influence Interpersonal Effectiveness

Listen. Often easier said than done. Too many people do not practice the skill of listening because they have never had any training and don't know or understand the techniques involved. If this is true for your team, consider some short-duration training to help your group understand *how* to listen.

Create situations where everyone wins. This is the heart of negotiating. As the team works through the issues related to its problem, it is important that all members feel that they have been heard and that their ideas are integrated into the solution—this is the WIN you are seeking.

Be open to new ideas. Problem solving frequently involves paradigm shifts. There are exercises and techniques that can be used to expand the lateral thinking capacity of team members. Develop shared team reminders to keep the team out of thinking ruts.

Be positive. Thinking positively is a discipline. Each member must take responsibility for thinking positively—reaching for solutions—rather than focusing on what is wrong with the current situation or someone's idea.

Stay focused. A way to achieve this is through the use of agendas. These can be considered a team tool to keep the group on track. Lack of focus can also be caused by lack of leadership, unclear mission, lack of buy-in into the problem being addressed. Each team member has the responsibility of helping to keep the group focused and to calling attention when diversion is occurring.

Strive for consensus. Problems that are addressed through a structured problem-solving team are generally ones that are important to the organization and that impact many individuals. As a consequence, those involved must truly support the resolution—this is best accomplished when the group agrees by consensus to any action it takes. Allow extra time for this process. It takes time for all to be heard and for buy-in to occur. Be sure the team agrees that the problem is important enough.

Focus on the problem. When a team is working through problem solving, it is easy to stray from the problem, and instead, begin to focus on people in the group. Remember your goal is to attack and solve the problem, not to attack people in the group.

Perceptions are reality. Recognize that a person's opinion or perception is reality to that person and that it may not match your reality. There can be as many perceptions of reality to any problem situation as there are people on the team.

A sample guideline form is shown below. Your team can use this when creating your own list of guidelines. A blank form is included in Appendix C, Page 193.

Our Team Guidelines

As a team, we have decided that these are the guidelines we will follow for all problem-solving sessions. Each team member is responsible for behaving according to these agreed-to guidelines.

- *LISTEN—don't interrupt*
- *Ask questions when we don't understand*
- *Be on time to meetings*
- *Stay focused on the task*
- *Follow the process outlined*
- *Respect the timekeeper*
- *Be open to suggestions*
- *Be positive*
- *Listen as an ally*

PROCESS CHECK—HOW WILL WE MONITOR OUR PROGRESS?

As your team works to accomplish its task (solve the problem), it is important that you periodically check to see how the group is operating. If you think of yourselves as a car moving between two points, the process check is the equivalent of taking time to check the oil, put in gas, and do maintenance to see that the engine continues to run so you can complete your journey (the task). A team process check includes checking up on the group's problem-solving and interpersonal processes. Ask questions that focus on how the group feels it is progressing with the assigned task and on the relationships among team members.

Trap:	Focusing only on the group's task and ignoring the interpersonal issues, while still expecting to produce a high-quality product.
Solution:	Use a Process Check periodically (usually at milestone points within the project), on a regularly scheduled basis (at the end of each session or group of sessions), or whenever the team needs an opportunity to express how they are working together.

We recommend doing a short, informal interpersonal check at the end of each meeting and periodically, using a structured checksheet or assessment instrument to measure group process. Allow a few minutes at the end of each session to review your interpersonal process. People working together harmoniously is not a lucky happenstance. The entire team must work to achieve the maximum possible benefit from each other's contribution to the team's output. As you develop skills in group process, you may choose to use different measures of your team's progress.

Your group can decide who will be responsible for monitoring group process. Recommended approaches:

1. Give the facilitator the responsibility for watching process, reporting on it, and guiding group discussion during meetings and working sessions.
2. Survey the team to determine how individual members perceive team interaction. This process surveying can be done:

   - Verbally—using a key question that is asked of everyone.
   - Via free-form discussion or question asking (written or oral).
   - Using a structured questionnaire.

Anything verbal requires more group trust. If you don't feel your team is ready, use some form of checksheet that lists key questions about individual and team behavior. If trust levels are low, do this process check anonymously. Ultimately the goal is open communication among team members; that is, sharing feelings about meeting process without the need for secrecy.

Tool Description

Verbal process checks: these use one or two key questions that the group discusses. Examples of questions:

- What did you like about today's meeting?
- What is something the facilitator/leader should know (this can be a pat on the back or a critique)?

- What should we do differently at our next meeting?
- What was most important to you personally in today's meeting?

As you can see, the questions are getting at the positive and negative aspects of the meeting. You can round-robin your discussion or have people offer ideas at will. Whichever option you choose, be sure that all team members contribute their ideas—pull out from quiet members if necessary. Another option is to use the whip technique. To do this, present the question and quickly go around the group having each member state his or her immediate reaction to the statement. Because the discussion is minimal—simply stating a thought about a topic—it is a quick technique that can be used to evaluate your meetings. The last five minutes of any meeting should be dedicated to reviewing your process.

Free-form discussion: This option relies on open-ended questions. Each team member answers a series of questions, usually three to five. The questions are designed to encourage members to share whatever they think about the team's process. Examples of questions:

- How do you feel about our meeting agenda expectations?
- What are some things we could do to make our meeting process better?
- What do you like most about our meetings?
- What advice do you have for the team leader/facilitator— things that would improve the quality of our meetings?

These questions can be answered in a variety of ways. The analysis of the data collected can be a little more difficult because of the lack of structure. However, the information can be very insightful; and it is an excellent way to capture *different* ideas that can be incorporated to improve process. See the Team Process Check on page 31.

Be sure to make someone responsible for seeing that something happens as a result of the information supplied by team members.

Structured questionnaire/checksheet: This option takes the most effort to construct and can provide very specific information about certain aspects of team process. Approximately 10 questions are included in the survey—statements can change over time as you focus on different aspects of team relationships. Team members

---

Team Process Check—Short Form

Each team member is to complete the statements below. The team facilitator will then lead a group brainstorming/discussion around each item. The focus is on process **not** individuals—the input is about what was happening in the last session, not about individual team members.

What did you like most about today's process?

_____

_____

What would you like to have had occur differently—and how?

_____

_____

What would you like more/less of in future sessions?

_____

_____

---

simply answer yes/no or circle a number on a scale to reflect their feelings. Survey responses can include names or be anonymous. Answers can be tabulated at the session and discussed immediately, or the discussion can be the first agenda item for the next meeting. Most groups use a facilitator for the discussion, especially if there is any degree of disagreement in responses. Examples A and B are two kinds of assessment instruments. Duplicable copies are included in Appendix C.

Example A

Team Process Check—Long Form

Each member is to answer the questions below, and the team is to discuss responses. Reviewing process allows the team to share perceptions—all

perceptions are accurate for the individual providing the view. Focus on listening
to input and asking constantly, "How can we use what we hear to make our
process better than it currently is?" The Comments column can be used to record
anything that needs to be followed up on.

Group Question	Yes/No/ Somewhat	Comments
1. Did the meeting follow the planned agenda?	_____	_____
2. Were no more than 10 minutes (if that much) spent on review and warm-up activities?	_____	_____
3. Was time used effectively?	_____	_____
4. Was there encouragement to participate— were all members comfortable sharing their views?	_____	_____
5. Were useful ideas generated?	_____	_____
6. Were people open to ideas of others—did we LISTEN to each other?	_____	_____
7. Did the group attempt to reach consensus on important decisions?	_____	_____
8. Did we follow our team guidelines?	_____	_____
9. Are we following the problem-solving steps?	_____	_____
10. Is the team using the problem-solving tools appropriately?	_____	_____
11. Are all team members volunteering for various team roles and action items?	_____	_____
12. Is everyone completing team assignments—on time and in a quality way?	_____	_____

Example B

Team Assessment Instrument

What I say is	What I say is
listened to with	ignored or not
attention / respect	heard.

|___ 6 ____ 5 ____ 4 ____ 3 ____ 2 ____ 1 ____|

The listening referred to in this statement is the nonverbal and verbal interaction between team members. Key listening skills that should be demonstrated by all team members include:

- Taking responsibility for maintaining an interest in what the other person is saying—this will be reflected through **active listening.**
- Assuming responsibility for making sure that you understand what the other person is saying—this is demonstrated by **good questioning.**
- Clarifying what you heard to be sure that you received an accurate message, not one influenced by your perceptions or biases. This reality check is done when each person **paraphrases** what was heard before contributing new ideas.

What I say is prized	What I say is
and valued here.	discounted or
	belittled.

|___ 6 ____ 5 ____ 4 ____ 3 ____ 2 ____ 1 ____|

This question reflects a second level of listening. It is more than hearing the other person and practicing good listening skills; it refers to the issue of respect among team members. People tend to feel more comfortable discussing facts and opinions than they do discussing values and beliefs. However, it is this deeper discussion and corresponding listening that determines team effectiveness. Only when members value each other as human beings, will

they respect the input and contribution of each member. Valuing
is necessary if the team is to be able to deal with difficult problems.

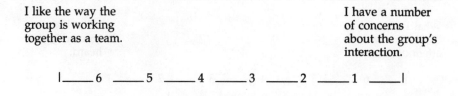

I like the way the   I have a number
group is working   of concerns
together as a team.   about the group's
                                                            interaction.

|____ 6 ____ 5 ____ 4 ____ 3 ____ 2 ____ 1 ____|

This references the maturity of the team—it is into Stage 3 or 4
of the team development model. The group is able to focus on
producing a quality solution, is not hampered by interpersonal
conflicts among members, and has a camaraderie that is beyond
just getting the work done.

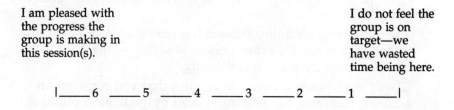

I am pleased with   I do not feel the
the progress the   group is on
group is making in   target—we
this session(s).   have wasted
                                                            time being here.

|____ 6 ____ 5 ____ 4 ____ 3 ____ 2 ____ 1 ____|

This focuses on the mechanics and content of the problem-solving
endeavor. The group is moving through the model in a timely
manner.

> You have completed the setup steps that help team-based problem
> solving run smoothly. You are now ready to begin addressing
> your team's problem.

SCENARIO (*continued*)—*Step 1*

The Takeout problem was the perfect opportunity to try out team-based problem solving. Mary suggested to Jan that they ask four of their employees to form a problem-solving team that would use the *Team-Based Problem Solver* to look at the drop in Takeout revenue.

Meeting 1

The next day Mary purchased four copies of the *Team-Based Problem Solver* and met with the selected team members: Tim, the line cook, Tina, the hostess/cashier, Mae, the lead waitress/cold prep, and Michael, the manager-in-training. She told them that a solid Takeout business was critical for the restaurant's long-term business success. She isn't sure if the current drop in revenue is an aberration or a symptom of a major problem, and she shared that Jan and she can't afford to ignore this signal.

She stated that she was looking forward to each of their contributions to solving the problem. They discussed the benefits and barriers of solving problems in teams. Mary indicated she would try to make as much time available for them to meet as she could by reshuffling some staffing schedules, and she told them to let her know if they needed any additional resources. She couldn't promise, but she would try to meet their requests. She said that once they had identified the key causes, she wanted to meet with them to determine the next steps. Their current charge is to identify the reasons why the revenue has dropped. She reviewed the Problem-Solving Model with them and the Getting Started Section. She suggested that they review the entire guide before their first meeting. A one-and-a-half hour meeting was set for the next afternoon.

Meeting 2

At 2:30 the next afternoon, the four team members got together. They started out by looking at the Process Road Map material. Mae mumbled that she thought it was a lot of hogwash. Tina said she thought it might be helpful, that in her church they had used some similar material, and it had been very constructive. Tim agreed, saying they had to do similar things at the self-help meetings he attended. Michael said he was pretty enthused about all the tools and techniques.

Tina suggested they begin by developing the agenda for the meeting. Everyone agreed. They posted the agenda on a flip chart:

```
                        Agenda
        Roles                       10 min.
        Team Guidelines             20 min.
        Step 2 Intro                30 min.
        Process Check               5 min.
        Develop next agenda         10 min.
```

Everyone wanted Michael to be the leader. He made it clear that he would do it this time, but said that just because he was a manager didn't mean he should be the team leader. Tina suggested that they review the section on leadership, pages 19–24 and independently complete the questions asked.

After a brief discussion, they decided that they were defining the leader role interchangeably with the facilitator role. Mae said she still didn't understand what the difference was between the roles. Tim started to explain it to her again, however Tina interrupted, suggesting they just use the team leader as everyone was familiar with it. Everyone agreed. They also agreed to taking turns fulfilling the various roles. After discussion, the team decided on the following role assignment for the meeting:

```
        Role Assignments
        Michael—Leader
        Tina—Scribe
        Mae—Timekeeper
        Tim—Gatekeeper
```

Michael agreed to serve as contact for the duration of the project.

They moved on to team guidelines. Using the affinity diagramming process explained in Appendix A, the group reviewed the guides in Getting Started and modified it into a list of guidelines that they felt would be critical for their team to be effective:

Our Team Guidelines

As a team, we have decided that these are the guidelines we will follow for all problem-solving sessions. Each member is responsible for behaving according to the guides:

- *LISTEN—don't interrupt*
- *Ask questions when we don't understand*
- *Be on time to meetings*
- *Stay focused on the task*
- *Follow the process outlined*
- *Respect the timekeeper*
- *Be open to suggestions*
- *Be positive*
- *Admit when we don't know something*
- *Enjoy working together*
- *Keep a sense of humor*

Michael said they'd now move on to step two: preparing the problem and the group. Mae said it was about time. She also informed them that they were now 15 minutes behind schedule. Michael said he'd shorten the next section to 20 minutes and suggested that Mae give him a five-minute warning. Tim rolled his eyes. Michael ignored Tim and asked everyone to turn in their guides to step two—Preparing the Problem. (*To be continued on page 46.*)

Step Two

Preparing the Problem and the Group

GOAL: Clarify the issue and gain agreement on the problem to be addressed.

Getting started	Preparing the problem and the group	Interviewing the customer	Analyzing	Creating the best solution	Implementing the best plan	Monitoring results

Surface the Problem
Define the Problem
Develop the Problem Statement
Assess Readiness to Move Forward

SURFACE THE PROBLEM

Problems can be identified by anyone involved in the process. Typically, managers, customers, or team members themselves are aware that a problem exists because of their involvement in the process. The key is to raise the awareness to action. Avenues must be available within the organization for the surfacing of problems.

Think back. What did you do the last time you were aware of a problem in your organization? Did you:

1. Initiate action yourself to address the problem?
2. Use a mechanism that is in place in your organization to assure that problems surface and are dealt with?
3. Talk to key people to alert them to the problem, so they could initiate appropriate action?
4. Think that there was a problem and hope that someone with power would do something about it?

In successful problem-solving cultures, items 1 through 3 are the norm and 4 is not permitted.

Regardless of who surfaces the problem, the team must take ownership of it in order to seek resolution. This is critical because effective problem solving does take energy and time. Unless the team feels strongly that there is a problem (what it is and how important it is), core problem solution will be unlikely.

DEFINE THE PROBLEM

Once you have isolated the problem that your team will be addressing, your first task is to describe your problem so that each member of the team has a clear picture of its parameters. To define the problem, you will need to develop an understanding of what is currently happening. Ask yourselves: What are the characteristics of the situation we face? What kinds of information do we need in order to understand the problem situation?

List the information you think will be necessary to fully understand the current situation—do this individually:

_____

_____

_____

_____

_____

As a team review your lists. Then brainstorm any additional information you need to clarify and understand fully the problem situation.

Trap:	Accepting a perceived problem as fact. A customer, a manager, or a team member emphatically states what the problem is and may even provide data that appears to support the assumption. The tendency is to see the person as the expert and accept his or her definition.
Solution:	Verify all information, and collect additional data to fully describe all aspects and characteristics of the problem. Don't let rank, individual expertise, or someone's over confidence substitute for good data: • By using the problem-solving tools provided, such as the **5 W's and H** or **Brainstorming** (see Appendix A), a team can take the focus off individuals and place it on the data-collection process. Use these tools to help your team develop lists of information you need.

Trap:	Jumping ahead to solution-oriented information. Before a team has even begun to understand the current situation, they are gathering data on what they can change, modify, and improve.
Solution:	Always check to ensure that the data describes the current state of affairs. When you hear yourselves asking, "Can we, Will you, How can we, What if?" you are generating or seeking solution data. • Maintain focus on gathering ideas, not solving problems or being concerned with issues that prove divisive.

As you define the problem, be sure your team focuses on why you are working to solve the problem: You want to improve the quality of some aspect of your operation, which will result in a better product and/or service for your customers. In almost all cases, the problem you are working on must be recognized by your customer as a priority and result in a value-added activity for your team.

Trap:	Choosing a problem that will improve your internal quality, but that currently does not have a high priority with your customers. Many companies failed in their early quality efforts because they selected problems that they felt comfortable with and that subconsciously allowed them to continue to avoid or to have limited contact with their customer. Even though significant savings and improvements were seen, they still lost market share and/or continued to have major customer problems because they were not addressing issues that were highly important to their customers.
Solution:	Make sure the problem you select will meet a current customer need by validating its importance with your customers. This means *ask* them; *talk* to them. Don't accept at face value someone else's opinion that it's important to your customer.

Once your team has identified what it thinks the problem is, you are ready to do more investigation to be sure you have indeed identified the core problem that needs to be addressed and not some symptom that parades as the problem. You might do some preliminary brainstorming around potential causes of the problem as you have thus far defined it. Focus on identifying areas about which you will need more information.

DEVELOP THE PROBLEM STATEMENT

Your problem statement should be short and simple. People who are unclear about what they are trying to solve tend to ramble. The problem-solving process requires that you focus on core issues, and these can usually be stated succinctly. If your problem statement has more than two sentences, you probably have more than one problem. (Other ways of acknowledging succinctness—A problem statement in 25 words or less. A problem statement in no more than two lines of writing.)

As you develop your problem statement, focus on describing the issue in terms of an *undesirable, verifiable* event. Ask yourself what is happening that you don't want to continue to happen. Examples: Our customers' problem is that 30 percent of their calls are not returned within a 24-hour period or: Our problem is that it takes us 15 days to process accounts receivable.

Verify that you have identified the root problem by checking your problem statement against the *why criteria*. Example: Why are 30 percent of the calls not returned within 24 hours? If you can answer that question based on whatever data you have about the current situation, it is not the core problem statement. When you reach a point at which you can no longer answer the *why criteria*, you have arrived at the core problem.

Trap:	Describing the problem in terms of a desired performance target or solution. Teams at this stage of the process tend to be reluctant to describe a *negative* situation so they couch their statement in terms of expected performance.
Solution:	Do not imply a solution or desired performance target in your problem statement. Describe the undesirable condition, event, circumstance. Let your data be your voice. Remember that this is a starting point. As you verify your data with your customers and begin to analyze the causes of the problem, you may have to revisit your problem to further clarify or refine it.

In the space below, write a statement of the problem your team needs to resolve:

_____

_____

_____

_____

_____

Do other team members agree with you? Discuss each member's statement and then write a preliminary problem statement that all team members agree is in the ballpark. Enter the team's preliminary statement in the box provided on page 60 in Step 3—Interviewing Customers.

Trap:	Arguing about the issue or goal of your group. Too often a team can lose sight of its real purpose by *wasting time* arguing.
Solution:	Keep the focus on understanding each member's view and achieving consensus: • Consensus means committing to support the group's action or decision. It does not mean that there has to be a 100 percent agreement on the topic. • To do this, focus on *listening*. Ask open-ended questions that generate information about why an individual thinks a certain way. Identify the frame of reference being used. • Use a consensus-building tool such as multivoting or nominal group technique (see Appendix B).

> If for some reason your team cannot reach agreement about what the problem is, bring in an outside facilitator. It is the responsibility of this person to determine if the team has identified truly distinct problems that need to be addressed separately or whether the group needs assistance in developing its team skills. If it is determined that separate teams should be formed, do so and then return to the beginning of the process with each newly formed team.

ASSESS READINESS TO MOVE FORWARD

Once you have solidified your problem and thought a little about potential causes and the time and energy it will take to gather the information, you will need to decide on your readiness to actually deal with the problem. A Problem-Solving Readiness Survey will help your team determine if you should get involved with the problem-solving process—now, in the future, or at all. Each of the questions in the survey addresses an aspect of the process that influences whether your team will be successful. Groups sometimes start out with the best of intentions about solving a problem but hit a roadblock once they get into the actual process—this frustrates the team members and hinders future attempts at dealing with the problem.

The five survey questions are listed below. A complete explanation is included in The Problem-Solving Readiness Survey in Appendix B, page 167.

1. Is your team ready and able to act on the issue you have identified?
2. Is at least one member of your team positioned to have the **power to authorize** any action you may determine to be necessary to solve your problem?
3. Do you have the best people to work on this problem?
4. Have you identified/included all individuals whose input will be required in the problem-solving process—for the entire project and as interim "subject experts"?

5. Is there a system in place to obtain appropriate sign-off at the various stages of the process?

Trap:	Trying to solve problems that you are not equipped for. You must have the right conditions and people in place if your team is to successfully address an issue. Don't let egos and position power get in the way of the team's deciding whether to, and who should, address the given problem.
Solution:	Determine if the team can get to "yes" for each question. Through group discussion—use a facilitator—analyze your group's situation: What caused members to answer no? If you are basically the right team to solve the problem, develop action plans that will assure that you get the resources—including people—that you need to move ahead. If you decide you are not the right team, think corporately. Take responsibility to see that those who should be involved are—or, at least, report your findings to those with the power to take action. Being able to say no to a presented problem takes courage. It helps when you can back up your statement with factual reasons for your decision and some ideas on who should be charged with addressing the problem and why.

Once you have decided you are ready to proceed, take the time to read through the problem-solving model in its entirety before you begin to deal with your actual problem. Understanding the entire process can help you decide what types of guidelines might be needed at different stages of the process. Taking the time to read now allows you to prepare ahead of time. You can plan for and collect the information you will need along the way before it is needed and prevent unnecessary time lags. Reading also helps you gain a big-picture view of where you intend to end up and can prevent unnecessary detours. An additional part of readiness means having individuals in place who are willing to support the process in an unqualified manner. Team members must agree to demonstrate supportive behaviors as a way of following the leader they have selected. This represents the other half of the team contract. A leader should be able to expect a team to provide the support they jointly identified as being appropriate.

> **Until the entire team is comfortable with the following paragraph, you should proceed no further.**

At this point, your team is clear as to its purpose—what the problem is that we are here to solve. And the team has established some operational guides that will allow it to focus on the content that must be addressed. Potential process issues have been identified. Techniques for dealing with any interpersonal issues that might arise have been proactively identified, and plans for addressing them have been spelled out to the satisfaction of the entire team.

TIME FOR A PROCESS CHECK!

SCENARIO (continued)—Step 2

Meeting continued

The team clarified the issue they were to address and wrote it on a flip-chart sheet that would be posted throughout the problem-solving activity:

> **Issue:** Takeout orders dropped significantly over the last six weeks (mid September through the end of October)

Then they reviewed the instructions for brainstorming. On the flip-chart they wrote the question: What information do we need to clarify and fully understand the problem? The following list of potential causes and needed information was generated using brainstorming:

Flip-Chart 1	Flip-Chart 2
Info needed	*Info needed*
Severity of the problem	% of sales drop
One-day drop or over-time drop?	Quality of food
Poor produce this month	Wrong orders
Orders ready on time?	Hot food cold
Cold food hot?	Time from order to delivery
Time from restaurant to customer	Getting through on phone
Weather	Construction in area
Pattern of revenue drop	Business shutdowns
Equipment failures—ours/theirs?	Delivery problems
Busy order taker	Flu bug going around
New competition	Limited menu
	Rude order taker

The team reviewed their brainstormed list and discussed it. They were surprised by the number of different things that might have impacted the drop in orders and that would potentially have to be looked at. Some of the information was already known. Mae and Tim said the produce was not as good as it had been with the old supplier. Mae reminded the team that according to the agenda, they had five minutes left for this discussion. Tina said that a new Chinese takeout restaurant had opened a couple of blocks over. She also didn't think the problem was in the order taking because the restaurant's phone system allowed people to leave messages; however, the group decided they shouldn't eliminate order taking yet. Tim mentioned that many of the potential causes focused on delivery and that the team was not really familiar with that area. He suggested they add Danny to the team. Danny is the storeroom clerk and drives the delivery truck. Michael said he'd ask Jan about adding Danny and he also would gather the financial data. Tina noted that most of the brainstormed items fell into a few main categories: delivery, food quality, service quality, financial trends, environmental factors, and marketing issues.

Mae announced that it was time to do a process check. Michael suggested that each member share their responses to these two items: "What I liked about today's meeting," and, "What would make the next meeting better?"

	Liked	*Better*
Michael -	Everyone participated	Sticking to the agenda
Mae -	Lots of ideas	Starting on time
Tim -	Using the guide	Less interrupting
Tina -	Getting to know each other	More participation

The team completed the agenda form (see below) and agreed to review their brainstormed list with the other workers, collecting as much data as possible.

Agenda

Team: TOOT (Take Out Order Team)   Date: 11/5

Time—start: 2:30   end: 4:00

Location: Conference room

Leader: _____   Timekeeper: _____

Facilitator: _____   Scribe: _____

Purpose: Review data that has been collected so far.

Meeting preparation: Background/Premeeting assignments:
Review brainstormed list with co workers.

Please bring: Supporting data

Agenda Item	Responsible Person	Process to Address Topic	Time	Expected Outcome	Actual Outcomes*
Warm up	Tina	Discussion	5 min.	revised agenda that all agree to	
Assign Roles	Mae	Group Discussion	10 min.	know who is doing what in meeting	
Review Collected Data	Michael	Group Discussion/ Brainstorming	1 hr	fairly comprehensive list of problem causes	
Set next agenda	Tim	Discussion	5 min.	next meeting's agenda	
Process Check	Tina	Process check questions	10 min.	some idea of how the team feels about the process so far	

End of meeting planning:

Evaluation technique/process: Will need to get process questions ready for meeting.

Action to be taken: Michael will check with Jan about having Danny participate on the team.

*To be filled at the next meeting to be sure that there are no unfinished items and to document actions agreed to.

Meeting 2

At the next meeting, Danny joined the group. He was really excited about participating and wanted to make sure all his issues got on the list—late supplier deliveries, lack of storeroom space, lack of a second driver for catering, problems with supplier payments, and so on. Tina nicely interjected that it might be helpful to revisit the stated problem to see if all these issues were relevant to the problem the team had been asked to address. Mae said that everyone she had talked with was convinced that if she could hire another prep person to do the catering prep, the food and service quality issues would be solved. Michael thought the greater need was for an additional delivery person and a second truck. Mae disagreed strongly. Tim mentioned that the restaurant was losing the construction-worker business to a roadside catering operation that had recently moved into the area, and he felt the second truck was a good idea that would allow the restaurant to stay even with the competition.

Tina again interjected, reminding everyone that the group's current task was not to solve the problem but to gather data so they could clearly define it. She suggested that the team quickly review the agenda and move on to the second item. Assigned roles could help the team use the available hour-and-a-half most efficiently. The team guidelines were posted on the wall and roles were assigned:

```
          Team Roles
    Tina—leader
    Tim—timekeeper
    Mae—scribe
    Michael—gatekeeper
```

Danny asked where the team guidelines came from. They realized that Danny would need to be brought up to speed and have an opportunity to give his input on the topics discussed the day before. Tina adjusted the day's agenda to include ten minutes for Danny's data. Michael suggested that roles for the next meeting be decided at the end of a meeting when the agenda was put together. He noted from his past experience as leader that an effective leader read ahead and was prepared to lead the group through a step. Everyone agreed and a few extra minutes were added to the agenda-setting time.

Michael then asked everyone to share the additional data they had collected from their co-workers. After reviewing the data, it was evident that many had been aware that a problem was developing but there was no clear indicator what the problem was. Michael shared the financial data he'd gotten from Jan. He noted that a definite trend could be seen. Beginning in late August, a little revenue had been lost each week. By October the business was posting a 5 percent loss each week, resulting in a 20 percent drop for October. If the trend wasn't halted by year-end, Takeout revenue would be significantly below projection. The team agreed that the problem they were addressing was very serious and needed some quick in-depth analysis.

Since the reason for the drop in customer takeout orders was unclear, the group decided to define their problem as the drop in revenue. It would at least give them a starting point. Using the guidebook criteria for developing a problem statement, they identified the problem as:

> *Revenue is dropping 5 percent per week resulting in a 20 percent loss in Takeout revenue for October.*

This statement was entered below the team's issue statement at the beginning of Step 2. As a group they were pleased with their increased understanding of what the problem really was. They were also beginning to understand how easy it would be to try to solve the wrong problem.

To celebrate their accomplishment they treated themselves to yogurt. Refreshed, they reconvened and were ready to move forward. "But first," Tina said, "when we rewarded ourselves with the yogurt, it made me think that we will need to remember to thank people who help us. How about if, whenever we think of someone to thank, we write their name and the reason on a Thank You Chart?" Everyone agreed although Tim thought they could remember without having to write a list on paper. Refocusing on the problem at hand, they quickly:

1. Completed the readiness survey.
2. Decided they were ready and that they were the right group to address this problem; however, they acknowledged a need to consider who else might need to be involved down the road.
3. Discussed next steps.

Tina summarized that from what the group had said, it was evident they definitely needed to interview some customers. The question was where to begin. She suggested that since each team member had talked to a number of different people, including a few walk-in customers, each should come to the next meeting prepared to identify the critical areas to collect information about. Michael requested that they think about how the team was going to gather data from customers. Danny didn't think more data was necessary. He said he knew the problem was late deliveries and that if another delivery person were hired the problem would be solved. Mae, Tim, and Tina simultaneously said, "We are not solving the problem—our goal is to understand it."

Michael quickly interjected, suggesting that delivery apparently was a key area to gather more data on and they could discuss how to do that at the next meeting. He said he felt really good about what they had accomplished so far. They had guidelines, a problem statement, an agreement that they had a clear charge, and an energetic team. Tina said she really enjoyed getting to know everyone else, Tim stated that he was learning a lot about the business, Mae said she had something to brag about at Bingo, and Danny was glad someone was finally paying attention to the problem he'd been bringing up for the last two months.

Tina began the wrap-up process:

1. She thought they had just done a process check, without being reminded!

2. She checked with the timekeeper and then suggested that they complete the next meeting's agenda and call it a day.

3. The team agreed that the more formal process check that Tina had prepared would be used at a later meeting.

4. Everyone agreed they needed to move quickly, so they decided to meet for two hours the next day.

5. Tim led the agenda-setting discussion.

(*To be continued on page 61.*)

Step Three

Interviewing Customers[*]

GOAL: *Determine who your external and internal customers are and what they expect from the process you are working on.*

Getting started	Preparing the problem and the group	Interviewing the customer	Analyzing	Creating the best solution	Implementing the best plan	Monitoring results

Identify the Customers Who Will Be Affected

Develop Interview Questions

Interview the Customers

Quantify Customer Concerns

Refine the Problem Statement

---

* Note: If you are addressing a problem that does not impact your final or external customers directly, you may not need to complete this step in its entirety. Some teams choose to begin using the problem-solving model by starting out with a very small, internally focused problem. This allows the team to focus on how they work together and on the model process itself without impacting external customer relationships. Understand however, that most problems, and especially those of any import, will require customer interface. If your team does choose an internal problem, do spend at least some time assessing the impact of the situation and its resolution on current customer satisfaction.

IDENTIFY THE CUSTOMERS WHO WILL
BE AFFECTED

As noted in Step 2, it is imperative that customer needs drive your problem-solving process. The first issue you face is identifying your customer. This is often much harder to do than you may think. In fact, many companies have failed in their early quality attempts because they could not clearly define their customer.

Here is a simple definition of the customer: a *person, or group, who receives an output (product, service, piece of information) from you.* However, the identification of the customer can be very complex if varying levels of internal and external customers are in your customer chain.

Before you begin your problem solving, you need to identify who are those who receive your output. It may be a person, department, or another business. Once you've identified this group, you need to validate that the issue you are addressing is important to them. Second, you must also determine if the issue will be important to their customers.

Frequently we are not fully aware of who the end customers are. A company that sells beauty products wholesale may argue over whether their customer is the drugstore-chain purchasing agent or the customer who buys their product off the drugstore shelf. The answer is both. They must be as aware of the needs of the end purchaser as they are of the needs of the purchasing agent. You, too, will need to consider all customers if your solution is to be successful.

If you are addressing a problem that is critically important to an internal customer, you must also validate that its solution will have a beneficial impact on the end customer. Many of today's large companies are experiencing severe business difficulties because they did not pay enough attention to the changing needs of their customer's customer.

Trap:	Arguing over who your customer is.
Solution:	If there is disagreement, assume that all individuals and groups mentioned are in your customer chain. As you gather data on their needs, it will become clear which are primary customers and which are secondary customers.

To effectively resolve your problem and improve process quality, you need to know what your customers expect and want. You may have internal customers or external customers or both who are affected by the process you are attempting to improve. Use the Customer Requirements matrix below to provide answers for each of the questions related to customers and their requirements:

1. Who are our customers? (List and then identify as internal or external.)
2. What service or product do we provide each one?
3. How important is the customer we've identified to the success of our organization? (Very, Somewhat, None or little)
4. How much would each customer identified benefit from this problem being resolved? (Very, Somewhat, Not likely)

Customer Requirements Matrix (Appendix B, Page 169)

Customer	Internal or External	Service/Product Provided	Importance*	Benefit*

*V = very important to the organization/beneficial to the customer.
S = of medium importance to the organization/benefit to the customer.
N = of no or minimal importance to the organization/benefit to the customer.

Key customers are those who receive a VV rating. If you have no VV ratings, reconsider the need to address this particular problem.

The customers identified as important are the ones to interview. Be sure they agree with your assessment of how much they will benefit by your addressing the issue thus far established as your problem.

DEVELOP INTERVIEW QUESTIONS

Once you have identified your customers, you need to find out how they see the service or product you are problem-solving around. Very often people assume they know what the customer is thinking—this can happen when you have very good relations, and it can also happen when your relationship is unsatisfactory. Assumptions are often wrong; therefore, it is important that you spend some time actually talking with the people you have identified as critical or representative customers. Your purpose is to gather some preliminary information about how your service or product is perceived. Keep the interview short; plan to come prepared with two to four key questions. This information will allow your team to begin your initial cause-and-analysis work.

Trap:	Trying to make this a "scientific study." Making your interviews too formal or difficult to conduct because you: • Are trying to collect too much information. • Are worried about the reliability or validity of your questions or what a single customer is telling you.
Solution:	Make your interview questions simple and open ended. The entire purpose is to generate information that will be valuable in the next steps.

Sample questions that you can use:

1. What service or product do you use? (Related to the process you are studying.)

2. Do we meet your expectations? (If yes, how? If no, why not?)

3. By what criteria do you judge our service or product?

4. What improvement or change would you like to see in our service or product?

Notice, all the questions are short and focus on what the customer likes about what you do or on what you can do differently to make your product or service better. Short questions let the customers tell you what they think is important—this is useful because it reveals perceptions about what you are doing. Later, when you are looking for causes of the problem, you will find that much of this information is outside your group's paradigm of the problem, and therefore is cause and solution expanding.

INTERVIEW THE CUSTOMERS

Face-to-face interviews (or telephone if distance precludes personal contact) should be conducted whenever possible. See Appendix A, Data Collection Methods for Surveying.

Trap:	Collecting biased data by having only the senior, experienced members on the team make contact with the customers.
Solution:	Having all members participate in the interviewing process will allow the data to be heard with a different ear. If you have a mix of experience on the team, have people pair up for the interview. This will allow junior people to participate, to learn interviewing skills from the senior people, and to contribute their perceptions of what the interviewee was saying.

Be open to what the customers are telling you—whatever they say is their perception of the service or product. Accept what they say with no defenses. Perception is reality. When you ask for information, don't try to influence the customer giving you the information—simply listen and take good notes. This is one of the benefits of having two people conduct the interview—you can compare notes about what was heard. If the two team members heard different messages, do more research to get at the true message.

Don't assume that the senior person's perception of what was said is the correct one. You want to incorporate the differing viewpoints into the team's discussion of driving causes.

Be sure to look for springboard questions—things the customer says that lead you to explore further. Techniques for exploring include, saying: "Tell me more." "Can you elaborate on that?" "I'm not sure I understand, can you help me with this?" The information you gather this way may not directly answer your original question, but it frequently garners relevant, important data. Sometimes information learned doesn't specifically address the problem you are currently solving, but it should be captured. It can be addressed in the future since it might reveal other problems—current or emerging.

Once the interviewing has been completed, your team is ready to organize and quantify the information collected.

QUANTIFY CUSTOMER CONCERNS

The first step is to determine what questions you need to ask around the data. For example, you might ask:

- What are some categories we can identify that describe what our customers have said about us?
- How often are certain things happening?
- What variables do we have—time, people, dollars, process, etc.?
- Are there any patterns to the data we collected?

The goal of your questioning is to quantify your customers' perceptions into facts—this is information you can problem solve around.

Checksheets are the simplest way to record your collected information. They are easy to understand and give you a clear picture of how often customers identified a certain problem area.

A sample is shown below:

Checksheet—Causes of Poor Service Provided by Dept. X

Day	Reliabil-ity	Response	Compe-tence	Courtesy	Access	Communi-cation	Understand Customer	Tangi-bles	Secur-ity	TOTAL
1	2	2	1		4	3	2	5	1	20
2	1	2		2	5	4	2	8		24
3	1	1	1		2	5	1	4	1	16
Total	4	5	2	2	11	12	5	17	2	60

The checksheet gives you a view of patterns in collected data. It doesn't take much energy to record the data or to analyze it. The key is to have the appropriate variables identified for counting.

Bar Charts are also a frequently used tool for displaying the relative importance of all the identified variables. They provide a visual display of the variables and their relative importance and help the team decide where its problem solving energies should be spent.

The height of the bar reveals the relative importance placed on a particular variable by those providing input. The concern most frequently stated will have the highest bar. This is frequently placed on the left side of the chart with each lesser concern placed to its right. This format is referred to as a **Pareto Chart**. See Figure 3–1. It is based on the 80/20 Rule of the 19th century Italian economist Vilfredo Pareto. Essentially the rule states that a few causes—20 percent—account for the majority of the problems—80 percent.

Bar-type charts are useful quantifying instruments because they give you a bird's-eye-view of the data you are dealing with. With a picture in place, you can move on to try to figure out what drives the data you have collected. A description and sample of a Pareto Chart is in Appendix B, page 170.

REFINE THE PROBLEM STATEMENT

You are now ready to move on. But first you must revisit the problem statement that you wrote after group discussion and agreement as part of Step 2—Developing the Problem Statement. Ask:

FIGURE 3–1
Pareto Chart (Histogram)—Causes of Poor Service by Dept. X

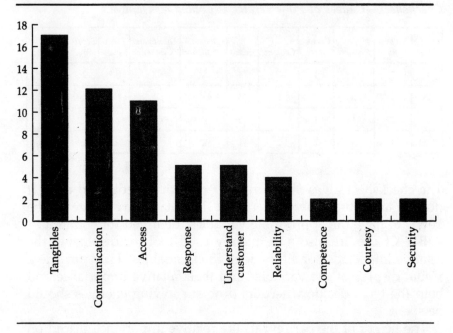

Did your customer substantiate what your team thought about the current situation? Did they shed new light on the situation?

Now that you have spent some time reality checking your statement with your customers and quantifying your data, go back, reassess, and discuss your problem statement.

> *Our Preliminary Problem Statement:*

Once the team agrees on the content of the problem statement, spend some time refining it. A refined statement can be read and understood by anyone. When you have finished refining your statement, enter it below.

> *Our Refined Problem Statement:*

TIME FOR A PROCESS CHECK!

SCENARIO (*continued*)—*Step 3*

Meeting 1

At the beginning of the next meeting, the team posted their guidelines and reviewed the agenda. Then they turned to Step 3 in *The Problem Solver* and followed the process for identifying customers. It worked pretty well. There was some disagreement over how to categorize customers, either by group: Walk-Ins, Phone Order—Delivered, Phone Order—Picked Up; or by type of customer: Office Worker, Construction Worker, and so on. They selected customer type for now, deciding they could segment by order type later. Their analysis showed that Office Worker was the critical external customer group, so they decided to focus their interviews on this group:

Customer	Internal or External	Service/Product Provided	Importance*	Benefit*
Jan & Mary	Internal	Analysis Report/Revenue	V	V
Office Worker	External	Take-Out Lunches	V	V
Construction Workers	External	Take-Out Lunches	N	V
Hotels & their Guests	External	Take-Out Breakfast & Lunch	S	V

*V = very important to the organization/beneficial to the customer.
S = of medium importance to the organization/benefit to the customer.
N = of no or minimal importance to the organization/benefit to the customer.

To determine the questions to ask this group, they reviewed the data they had generated in Step Two and added additional data they had since gathered. Using the multivoting technique described in Appendix B, which combines dot voting with consensus building, they identified the critical issues of Food Quality, Service Quality, and Delivery Issues to use as a basis for the customer interviews.

Next, the group needed to decide *how* to access the customers. The team shared their ideas. They brainstormed a list of potential scenarios but most appeared to be pretty random and time consuming.

At this point the team was getting pretty silly and unfocused. Even though they wanted to continue, they recognized that they had been at it for over two hours. Tina had been glancing at her watch for the last half hour as she was concerned about her child-care arrangements. Mae and Tim had already left twice to smoke. Michael was getting annoyed, but felt that as a potential manager if he said anything they might see him as flexing his management muscle. So, he suggested they call it a day. Mae, the session's leader, agreed. Danny, the gatekeeper, suggested they spend five minutes discussing the process questions Tina had prepared for the last meeting—what was helping their team work effectively and what things they needed to do differently. The ideas they generated:

Helps	*Improve*
Tools	Staying focused
Timekeeper	Not interrupting
All roles	Not jumping to solutions
Everyone contributing	Listening
Process checks	Sharing constraints with each other
Sense of humor	Check with group before leaving

Someone kiddingly said, "Hey, we can be another product the restaurant can market. We'll feed you and solve your problems." Everyone chuckled. All of a sudden Tim said, "Sounds like that marketing promo that we were doing a couple of weeks ago—Eat lunch with us and win a weekend of catered meals. You know, the one where we collected business cards for the drawing." Danny said, "Oh, I remember, I had a lot of catering that week so I was really crunched for time. I kept forgetting to ask people for their cards when I made the deliveries. Boy, some people really got bent out of shape." Tina excitedly interrupted, "That's it! We'll use those business cards to develop our interview pool. We saved them. Mary asked me to make a mailing list from them. We also noted which day we collected them. Besides getting general data we might also be able to see if our service varied from day to day."

Everyone was excited. It was a great idea. The team decided to meet right after the lunch rush the next day so that they could get started.

Michael stated that he knew some of the others had to leave so he volunteered to develop the agenda. He said he'd post it in the break room, and if anyone had additions or changes, to just make them right on it. He asked Tim to be the next day's leader and said he'd assign the other roles. Everyone thanked him and rushed out.

Meeting 2

The next day they did a quick agenda review and got right down to business. The team decided to do phone interviews supplemented by a few face-to-face interviews. Tina and Mae said that they would get some of the other front-of-the-house crew to assist them in making calls. Danny said he'd clean off the desk in the storeroom office, and they could use the phone there. Michael said he'd call a few longstanding customers and see if he could stop by. They decided to offer a free Takeout to those interviewed in person (not to exceed 10 lunches). When Michael delivered the takeout, he would interview them. The group had a budget of $75 from Mary. This plan fell well within the budget. Tim and Danny said they would informally query the customers they came in contact with.

Their goal was to poll at least 40 customers. The team determined that they would need one day to set up the interviews and two days to conduct them. They called Mary who agreed to staff an extra waitress on Thursday and Friday, so the phone could be monitored continually. She also agreed to take Michael's backup host/cashier position during the lunch rush on those two days, so that he could conduct the on-site interviews.

Following pages 56 and 57 in *The Team-Based Problem Solver*, they quickly developed the interview questions they would use.

> - *By what criteria do you judge us?*
> - *Do we meet your expectations for service, food quality, and timeliness?*
> - *Is there anything we could change that would improve our service to you?*

Danny, the timekeeper, said they had ten minutes left. Tim recommended they establish a timetable for the completion of the interviews, set the time and agenda for the next meeting, and do a quick process check. Danny volunteered to be the leader, Mae the gatekeeper, Michael the timekeeper and Tim, reluctantly, the scribe. Mae knew he was concerned about his spelling. She put him at ease, saying, "Tim, if you can read my scribbled order checks, I'll be able to decipher your notes." Tina spoke up, "Spelling isn't important, it's that we capture the information."

They used the Team Process Checklist Long Form for their process check.
It was a good wrap-up for the session.

Team Process Checklist Long Form		
Group Question Checklist	Yes/No/ Somewhat	Comments
1. Did the meeting follow the planned agenda?	S	Need an agenda check every 30 minutes.
2. Were no more than 10 minutes (if that much) spent on review and warm up activities?	Y	
3. Was time used effectively?	S	Stay even more focused. Leader bring us back on track.
4. Was there encouragement to participate—everyone was comfortable sharing their views?	Y	
5. Were useful ideas generated?	Y	
6. Were people open to ideas of others—did we LISTEN to each other?	Y	
7. Did the group attempt to reach consensus on important decisions?	Y	
8. Did we follow our Team Guidelines?	S	Monitor our interrupting. Listen to timekeeper. Ask questions for understanding.
9. Are we following the problem-solving steps?	Y	
10. Is the team using the problem-solving tools appropriately?	Y	
11. Are all team members volunteering for various team roles and action items?	S	It's okay to not be perfect speller, scribe, question asker, etc. Add to team guidelines—It's OK to not be perfect.
12. Is everyone completing their team assignments—on time and in a quality way?	Y	

The group left on a high note. They finally felt that they were making progress, though Danny still felt that the second truck was the answer.

Meeting 3

At Monday's meeting the team was anxious to sort through the data. Michael had already laid some of it out and was pinpointing key issues. Danny stated that three of the customers he'd talked to agreed with him that a second truck was a good idea. Tina suggested that before they got into the data, that they should follow the process road map and revisit the agenda. The group agreed. The agenda was reviewed and then Danny had everyone turn in *The Team-Based Problem Solver* to page 58, Quantify Customer Concerns.

The team decided that first they would group the customers by segment. They wanted to see if one group had more issues than another. They segmented the office worker population into three groups: Walk-Ins (12), Phone-order—pick up (12), and Phone order—delivery (16). For ease of capturing the information, they divided the data collection forms among themselves. Each person tallied the total number of issues identified on his or her forms. Tim then tallied the totals on a check sheet. It was evident that those receiving delivered service had the greatest number of issues.

Check Sheet—By Customer Segment

	Tina	Mae	Danny	Michael	Tim	TOTAL
Walk-in	2	0	3	1	4	10
Phone-order—pick up	8	5	5	8	4	30
Phone order—delivery	20	9	11	27	13	80
				TOTAL		120

Next they sorted the data by type of issues. The team developed the check sheet below to help them.

Check Sheet—Customer Complaints

	Late Delivery	Food Temperature	Food Quality	Missing Items	Wrong Order	Attitude	Order Taking Process	Order Pick-Up Process	Total
Walk-in	3	3	0	2	0	1	0	1	10
Phone-order—pick up	13	5	0	4	0	1	5	2	30
Phone order—delivery	26	28	3	12	3	4	4	0	80
Total	42	36	3	18	3	6	9	3	120

Since 66 percent of the total issues were identified by the Delivery customers, the team decided that they should address that data first. Referencing the Pareto Chart instructions in Appendix B, page 170, they constructed a Pareto chart from the data (see Figure 3–2).

FIGURE 3–2
Pareto Chart—Customer Complaints

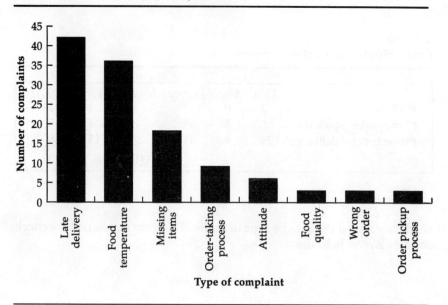

It was evident from their analysis that 80% of the complaints centered around late delivery issues, food temperature, and missing or substituted items. Mae guessed that at least 80% of the food temperature complaints were probably a direct result of the delivery being late. Everyone chuckled. Ever since the restaurant opened, Jan, the chef owner, had drilled into them that a simple definition of food quality was "hot food hot and cold food cold." Anything that interfered with that formula would automatically lower the food quality and impact customer satisfaction. Danny said, "I think the data proves that. Just looking through the responses it seems that almost every time someone complained about a late delivery they also noted food temperature or taste as a problem. I think there is a relationship." Michael said, "Let's check it out." He constructed the matrix shown in Figure 3–3. As suspected there was a definite relationship.

The team then revisited their problem statement. They realized that their original statement was a symptom of the problem, not the actual problem. They now felt they had enough data to define the problem through the eyes of their major customer—the delivery-service customer.

FIGURE 3–3
The Delivery/Quality Matrix

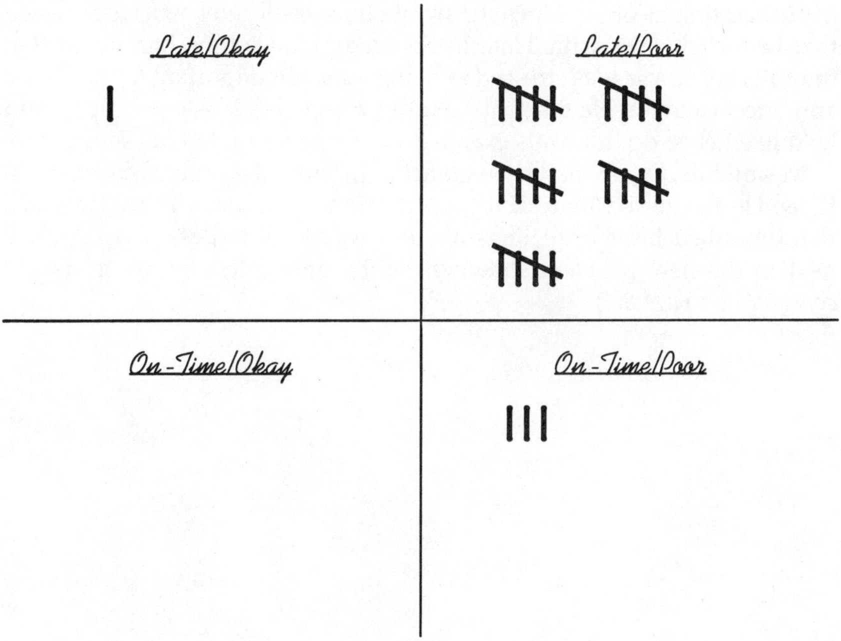

They recognized that there were other related problems that were also
contributing to the drop in revenue and that they would eventually need
to look at them, but it was evident that their starting point was late
deliveries. The statement they agreed upon was:

> *The problem is: Delivery service customers are experiencing
> a steady increase in receiving their meals late.*

They wrote the statement onto a flip-chart page and then mounted it over
their earlier, now incorrect, problem statement.

The team was ready to call it a wrap. However they had over a half
hour of scheduled meeting time left. Tina asked if the team could afford
to slack off now. She stated that they were finally ready to address their
initial charge: Identifying the causes of the problem. Tim shared with the
team that he had been glancing ahead in the book and that the next step
involved a lot of initial independent work. He suggested that maybe
everybody could complete it ahead of time. Thus the team could break
now, but not lose any time the next day. Everyone liked the idea and
agreed to it. Tim also said he'd put the next day's agenda together and
post it. He thought that had worked well the last time. Michael noted
that it was his time to be leader. He suggested they just repeat the roles
from their first meeting. Tim, who would have been gatekeeper, suggested
that he switch roles with Tina. In his reading ahead, he had noted that
the gatekeeper role was stressed as being critically important for the cause
and effect exercise. He felt that Tina did a superb job as gatekeeper, and
he'd like her to do it for this exercise. Everyone seconded his suggestion.

Meanwhile, Danny had been glancing through the process check questions. He suggested that each person write on a sticky note one word
that described his/her feelings about the process to date and mount it
next to the new problem statement as he or she left the room. (*To be
continued on page 80.*)

Step Four

Analyzing Causes

GOAL: *Thoroughly analyze all causes of the problem before beginning problem resolution.*

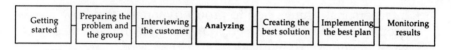

| Getting started | Preparing the problem and the group | Interviewing the customer | **Analyzing** | Creating the best solution | Implementing the best plan | Monitoring results |

Identify and Analyze Causes—Individual

Identify Causes—Group

Understand All the Causes

Determine the Root Cause(s)—Rank the Causes

Collect and Analyze Data on Root Causes

Trap:	Avoiding a disciplined approach to analysis and reaching a premature conclusion about the cause of your problem.
Solution:	Be sure to follow the process outlined in this chapter. It will help you avoid reaching a premature solution before you have unearthed all the possible causes and carefully analyzed feasible ones.

IDENTIFY AND ANALYZE
CAUSES—INDIVIDUAL

Once you have quantified your customers' major areas of concern, you are ready to begin to determine the causes of the issue your team intends to resolve.

A cause is the driver of the problem you see. Causes may be process or content oriented—that is, focused on how the work is being done or on what the work itself is. They may be:

- Personal (things tied to you or other individuals who are involved and reflective of intrapersonal issues).
- Interpersonal (things tied to group dynamics and how people work together, based in either human dynamics or work alignment dynamics).
- Organizational (tied to company hierarchy, culture, norms, ways of doing business internally and with customers).
- Reflective of values, conflicts, attitudes, a lack of skill or knowledge or time or energy, power conflicts, poor communication.

Begin by spending some time working independently. Your goal is to generate as many potential causes as you can for the problem your team is addressing. Write down all the causes you can think of—give yourself about five minutes for this initial, independent step:

_____

_____

_____

_____

_____

_____

You are now ready to go back through your list and categorize the causes you identified. Your goal is to come up with six or fewer categories into which all your causes will fall. Some general categories to consider (although not meant to be an exhaustive list, these are quite commonly used in problem-solving sessions): communication, procedures, materials, people, environment, equipment, training, and measurement. The categories you use should be broad enough so that a range of causes can logically fit together. You might use a matrix such as the one shown below for the categorizing process. List all your causes on the left, and then check those categories that are appropriate for your problem:

The Potential Cause Matrix—Individual Assessment (Appendix A, page 154)

Potential Cause	Communi- cation	Procedure	Materials	People	Environ- ment	Equipment	Training	Measure- ment	Misc.

Trap:	Thinking that you know how to use the tools presented within the text because they look familiar or seem self-evident in terms of how they are to be used. Some team members may not be comfortable in saying they haven't used specific tools before.
Solution:	Taking the time to read through the material in the Appendixes as a team before a tool is used for the first time. For some it will be educational because they haven't used many problem-solving tools in the past. For others, it will be a refresher and will allow all on the team to use a specific tool in the same way.

This approach allows you to visually check which categories predominate—all ideas in one or two categories would suggest that you *haven't removed your blinders* and you are only looking down a few paths for potential causes. You need to expand your thinking laterally to look for a broader range of potential causes. (See Appendix A—Creative Thinking Techniques, page 150.)

One technique you can use is questioning. Ask yourself some of the following "What if . . ." questions as a way of looking for other causes to the problem. You can insert as many modifiers as you wish—the following are meant to be thought provokers.

What if the cause were—reversed, inside out, smaller, larger, funny? Once you have identified all the potential causes you can think of based on your experience with, and knowledge of, the problem area, you are ready to share your causes with your team.

IDENTIFY CAUSES—GROUP

The team is ready to look for relationships between the effect (the problem the group identified) and its potential causes as identified by individual team members.

The fishbone diagram is a tool that is frequently used for the analysis process because it provides an easily understood visual representation of the problem and its associated causes. If you aren't familiar with how to construct a cause and effect diagram, also known as a fishbone diagram, check Appendix A, page 151 for instructions. Your goal is to identify *all* the causes you can— be sure to include all items identified by individual team members in the previous step. Categorize the problem causes on the fish. Add new categories as needed. Each team member shares his or her causes and indicates which category the cause belongs in. If someone disagrees, he or she can ask that a cause be entered in an additional category. Evaluating and critiquing is not allowed at this point in the process.

Critical judgment is crucial to problem solving but not during the idea-generating phase. For now, suspend critical judgment, focus on expanding through hearing and trying to understand the view of others. Create an accepting, inventive mood within your team—this is a time when the gatekeeper function is critical. It is the responsibility of this person to be sure that the group is open to all ideas, that all individual ideas are contributed to the fishbone, and that no one's ideas are censored.

Trap:	Creating a critical and competitive mood within the team by arguing during the idea-generation phase.
Solution:	Whenever there is a clear difference of opinion, do not waste time arguing. Rather, jot down the points that need more information or clarification—this can be done later. It may be that these represent ideas that need attention, but that are not a part of this particular problem.

UNDERSTAND ALL THE CAUSES

Once all the potential causes have been entered onto the fishbone, the group is ready to begin its critical thinking process. The team will be responsible for assessing all the causes that have been generated and for identifying the few that are probable, primary causes of the problem being addressed.

To assess the causes, it will be necessary to discuss each item in an inquiry mode. This implies a neutral beginning—I have no opinion about this particular item, I simply want to learn more about it—that allows the team to hear all opinions related to a specific cause. The goal of your questioning is to understand rather than to disagree. Ask a team member to illustrate her or his point and then use paraphrasing to reflect your understanding before you add thoughts of your own. This process relies heavily upon good communication skills—the role of the gatekeeper and/or the facilitator is to be sure that the team practices these skills.

Trap:	Not demonstrating good communication skills because the team either is not practicing them or lacks skill in this area.
Solution:	Before you begin your problem solving session, assess your team's communication skills. Look at past training that members have received and look at your past history of dealing with conflict. If you are weak in these areas, you can use an outside facilitator who can help you move through the problem-solving process and also educate you about group process as you proceed.

In team problem solving, difference of opinion is inevitable and healthy. In fact, such differences are important to the quality of the team's solutions. The reason differences occur is that each member is unique—we come to a discussion with a different *bag of history* (values, education, experiences, preferences, attitudes, etc.) and this is what drives how we perceive situations and the stands we take in discussions or conflicts. It is only when we can put all the views on the table and discuss them calmly, that we are truly able to determine the root causes of our problem.

A positive difference of opinion is constructive when it has as its goal, "I disagree and I want to find out why." Such a mind set is characterized by individuals who ask the following questions:

- Do I understand your viewpoint correctly?
- What assumptions or opinions or facts do you have that cause you to take that point of view?
- What information can we request from available resources to help us get a clearer, different perspective on the cause?
- What are the similarities between our two different opinions?

A difference of opinion will become destructive if it is:

- Taken personally by team members—most differences reflect team members seeing an issue from different perspectives, each equally valid in the eyes of the perceiver.

- Avoided issues that are swept under the table usually crop up at some time in a way that is destructive to the team's progress.
- Pursued in an exclusively argumentative mode by at least one team member—I disagree and must convince you that my view is the right one.
- Unresolved—just as with avoided issues, these will crop up in the future.

Some key communication behaviors that you can practice in order to facilitate the inquiry mode's effective operating include:

- **Paraphrasing**—repeat the meaning—not the exact words— so that individuals are able to correct each other's understanding of what was said about a particular item.
- **Questioning**—being sure to ask for more information about what was said as a way of clarifying. Don't assume you know what a person meant by a particular statement. Ask about assumptions, opinions, and facts—don't make value judgments about what others say.
- **Active Listening**—let the other person know through your nonverbal actions that you are listening to what is being said. Ninety three percent of your message is carried through your nonverbals.

DETERMINE THE ROOT CAUSE(S)—RANK THE CAUSES

The team is now ready to use *critical judgment* to evaluate the causes it generated. Its task is to identify the four to six root causes that are driving the problem.

During the process of analyzing root causes of the problem, the team needs to continually ask the following questions as each cause is discussed and weighed:

- Is this truly a cause or is it a solution?
- If it's a solution, can we turn this solution into a cause statement?

- Is this a symptom reflecting some underlying cause that we have not yet surfaced?
- If it's a symptom, can we identify the root cause?

Every time you can answer why something is occurring, you are identifying a symptom not a cause. It is only when the "Why" question cannot be answered that you have a true cause. The steps that the team will need to follow to determine the root causes are:

1. Clarify any causes you are not clear on. By this point you should have eliminated or restated symptoms or premature solutions.

2. Use some method of controlled voting once you have thoroughly discussed all the presented causes. You might consider using the cause filtering tool discussed in Appendix B, page 173. This technique provides the team with a voting mechanism that ranks the impact of causes on the problem's solution.

Trap:	Team leaders influencing the voting of team members—people watching each other before selecting their top causes.
Solution:	Quality solutions require honest, independent input. Each team member must focus on what she or he knows to be true—reflect what is true for your work unit and your customers. Create a climate that encourages and rewards different ideas. As a last resort, use a system of blind voting so that honest views are expressed—it can be easier to discuss anonymous votes, so that no one takes it personally. If you use this technique, consider it to be a beginning step—no team should have to continually use this approach. If you do, consider outside assistance to work through your blockage.

The team's goal at this point is to determine what it considers to be the potential key causes—the ones that if you do something about these, most of the problem will be resolved. (This is the Pareto principle—that 20 percent of the causes drive 80 percent of the effect.) Plan on identifying and exploring four to six root causes.

One technique for selecting the four to six root causes is to use the cause analysis matrix shown below. This type of analysis helps you decide whether you are positioned to deal with an identified cause. Sometimes we know what a cause is, and we realize that we can't do anything about it—we are the wrong people. At other times, you will have the power to address a cause directly because you have control of the resources and are in a position of power to deal with the situation. Frequently a team has some power or resources for addressing the issue, but must involve other stakeholders if real resolution is to occur. It is important to weigh out your ability to deal with a cause in relation to how important you consider the cause to be. If a cause is ranked very likely to occur and you have little or no control, you can do any of the following:

- Refer the problem to those who are positioned to deal with the cause and end your problem-solving efforts.
- Table the causes you can't deal with, identify those over which you have control, and continue your problem-solving efforts in those areas over which you do have control.
- Reconfigure your problem-solving team to include as a champion or active member someone who does have control over those causes you rank as most important.

Cause Analysis Matrix (Appendix B, page 175)

	We Have the Resources/Power to Address the Cause Directly			Our Customer Is Involved/ Impacted*		Individual	Consensus Generated
Cause	Yes	Somewhat	No	Yes	No	Ranking	Team Rank

* The customer column needs to be considered carefully. A *yes* response in this column indicates that your customer will need to be involved in some way in the problem-solving process if he or she is not already included. A *no* response means that you can move on without customer contact.

In today's workplace environment, very few problems will not involve or impact the customer in some way. Your team must decide just how involved you want or need your customer to be. Some options open to you include:

- Use the information you gathered through customer interviews as the basis for the ranking of causes.
- Make some internal assumptions about the customer's probable ranking—be careful of this option. When we assume we know what the other person is thinking we are often wrong.
- Move no further on the problem until the customer can be included in the process—invite the customer to participate on your problem-solving team.

The option you choose depends on the problem—its level of importance to the customer and the resources available to your team.

COLLECT AND ANALYZE DATA ON ROOT CAUSES

At this point your group should have a list of four to six root causes of the problem you are addressing. You are now ready to begin a process that will allow you to look analytically at what you think is causing the problem.

Trap:	Relying on *gut feelings* as a way of identifying the root cause(s). Sometimes we think we know a situation so well that we intuitively know the cause and/or we trust each other's knowledge so much, and are in sync, so we don't question our feelings or each other. An example of this was the Bay of Pigs Invasion—a classic example of *groupthink*.
Solution:	Forcing the group to spend some time gathering current data on what is occurring in the workplace regarding the causes we have identified. Gather information via the *simplest* method of data collection available to you before you begin your analysis of causes and selection of solutions.

The team needs to use an objective and simple means to determine if they have focused on the causes which will best solve the problem—especially in the eyes of the customer. The process should not be long or involved, but should provide the team with an indicator of the impact each possible cause has on the problem (remember the 80–20 rule). As suggested in the customer contact step, keep this effort simple. Put a time limit on this step and stick to it. There is often a tendency to think that we can get *just a little more* information that will be the heart of the matter.

Steps for Data Collection and Review

List the critical root cause(s) you want to explore—this is the list your team decided by consensus was the driver of the problem.

- Identify what information needs to be collected—what it is about the cause that you need quantitative data on, who or where it will come from.
- Select a method to collect the data—decide on a simple method that will allow you to get the necessary information. See Appendix A for a variety of data collection methods.
- Agree on time frames—how much time you will put into this effort. You want enough information to be sure you have a representative picture of the impact of the cause, but you don't want to put so much time into the activity that you lose track of the problem-solving process.
- Collect the data—include as many team members in the process as feasible.
- Create a visual representation of the data—graphs are used most commonly.

Once you have the data in visual format, the team is ready to discuss the collected data. This discussion should lead to consensus on which cause(s) has the greatest impact on your problem statement. It is, of course, easiest when a single cause emerges; this, however, isn't always the case, and you may need to explore two or three causes simultaneously.

TIME FOR A PROCESS CHECK!

SCENARIO (*continued*)—*Step Four*

Meeting 1

The next meeting began with a review of the agenda and process notes. They all chuckled over the item that said, "Understand sticky note that says, Push Me Pull You." This opened up a good discussion about how the members felt about the process to date. They shared how difficult it was sometimes to work within the process structure and keep track of a lot of data and group dynamics at the same time.

Tina suggested this might be a good time to complete The Team Assessment Instrument in Appendix C, page 198. She thought the team was at a good place to really discuss the group dynamics issues it addressed. Michael said this would mean an agenda revision and asked the group if that was OK. It was decided to skip the process check at the end of the meeting and do it here instead. Tim also suggested that they consider staying an additional 10 minutes. Everyone felt they could handle that. So 15 minutes was allotted for completing and discussing the process instrument. Tina agreed to facilitate the discussion.

It was a good exercise. In summary they felt they had made a lot of progress. They listened better, stayed more focused and really valued each other's input. A couple of them still felt the team could move faster and that at times the process seemed to be a hindrance. Tim said he'd felt that way early on in the process but was beginning to realize all the things that would have been missed if the process hadn't been followed. They decided that using the instrument was very helpful. Mae suggested they use it again after their presentation of causes to Mary and Jan.

The team was now ready to move on. Danny surprised the group by unveiling a six-foot fishbone he had created for the exercise (see Figure 4–1). His team members clapped and cheered. Jan stuck her head in and asked them to tone it down but said she definitely was looking forward to their report. Tim said they'd have so much information, she'd have to turn the dining room into a presentation hall! Mae suggested that they get to work.

Michael led them through the Fishbone exercise (Appendix B, page 151). They were amazed at the amount of data they generated. (See Figure 4–2.) A lot was similar but a great deal was unique.

Prior to discussing the causes, Michael asked everyone to read the section, Understand All the Causes starting on page 73. The ensuing

FIGURE 4–1
Fishbone Chart

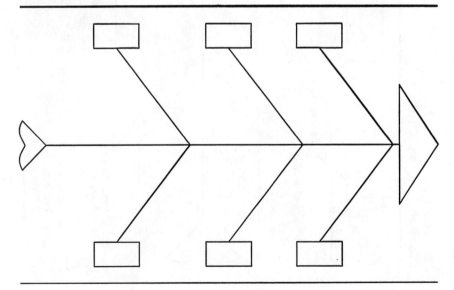

82

FIGURE 4-2
Completed Fishbone Chart

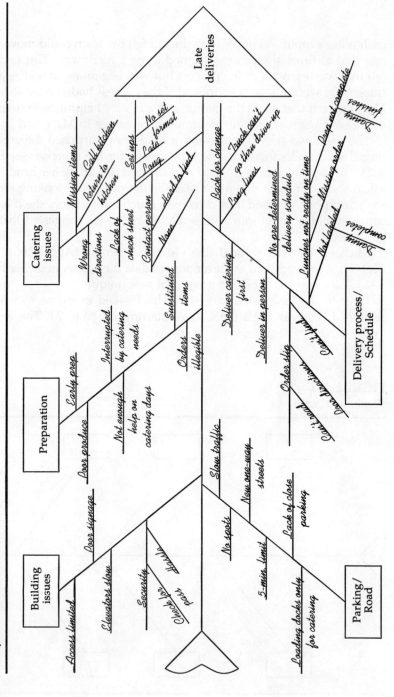

discussion of the causes went very well. Everyone listened carefully, asked good questions and really made an attempt to understand. They noted a number of relationships. Many causes seemed to be impacted by Catering and the lack of set procedures and guidelines.

When they were done, Mae said, "I'm exhausted, listening to really understand is hard work." Everyone agreed. Michael suggested they move to the counter for root beer floats and that they discuss the next day's agenda there. He heard no arguments.

The team agreed to use the Cause Filtering tool, Appendix B, page 173, to determine root causes. They would allow 20 minutes for screening and 20 minutes for ranking. They decided that depending on their results, they would use the rest of the time to prepare the presentation for Jan and Mary or to develop a plan to gather any additional data needed to analyze further a root cause.

Tina was the leader for the next day. She promised to review the information carefully because she realized how critical this part of the process was. She asked everybody to review the cause filtering tool before the meeting.

Meeting 2

At the next meeting, the group completed the Cause Filter. Tina cautioned them to stand up for their own beliefs and not to let others influence their vote if they felt very strongly about a potential cause. She suggested that they answer the likelihood question first for all causes and then answer the fixability question. This would help them see relationships and trends that might influence the vote on the easy-to-fix scale.

Michael reminded them that how easy something was going to be to fix might be heavily influenced by how much control they had over the situation. If parking in front of the building was a key cause, it probably would not be possible to get the city to reserve a parking space for the restaurant. Thus, alternatives would need to be explored. In answer to, How easy would it be to fix the parking problem?, Danny said it wouldn't be a problem if he could ride his bike like he used to. Tina told him to hold that thought until the next step, when solutions were considered.

When they completed the filter, Tina told them she now wanted them to identify the three to five key root causes, the ones contributing to at least 80 percent of the problem. The team discussed each V.V. category and then took a look at all those that were very likely to occur but would be harder to fix. This generated a lot of discussion. Mae agreed that it would be difficult to add an additional prep person, her solution to getting orders out closer to delivery; but if there was to be a complete solution to the problem, the group could not ignore the early prep issue. She reminded them that she currently prepped the fresh condiments for sandwiches at the beginning of her shift because on catering days she had to leave free time to assist in getting the catered dishes boxed up. Tim said, "You just identified that early prep is not a root cause, because you were able to state the reason you have to do it early. It's when you can't state a reason that we have a root cause." The team recognized that in answering some of the questions raised (i.e., generating promising solutions), they were beginning to position themselves for Step 5.

The team listed five key causes:

Key Causes

Catering operation given priority
Using truck for deliveries
Tightening of building access regulations
Illegible orders (sp?)
Lack of prep and set-up procedures for Catering
& Take-Out

Based on the key causes identified, Tina split the group in two. Half of them would complete the Cause Analysis Matrix in Appendix B, and the other half would identify additional data needed.

Using the information in Collect and Analyze Data on Root Causes in Step 4 pages 78–80 as a guide, Tina, Tim, and Danny discussed other data needed. They quickly zeroed in on the trend they thought they were seeing—that the growth of catering was the cause of the late deliveries and possibly many of the other problems that had been identified early on. The question was how to see clearly if there was a correlation.

They were discussing conducting more interviews so they could track the number of issues encountered on catering days versus noncatering days but were concerned about the time it would take. Tim remembered that when they had organized the data from the interviews, they had considered organizing it by days but then had opted for customer group. He asked if it still could be done. Tina said sure. The business cards had

FIGURE 4–3

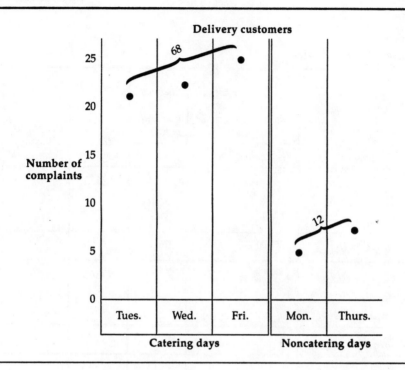

the dates of entry on them. Luckily she hadn't thrown them out and she had all the data collected to date. Tim then asked Danny if he could get the catering schedule for that week. The data could be sorted according to the number of issues identified by those who had a takeout delivery on a catering day versus those who received takeout on a noncatering day. In five minutes they had all the data they needed.

Plotting the data, they found a distinct relationship (see Figure 4–3).

Danny wanted to plot all the data but they were short on time. Tina suggested that it could be plotted later, if Jan and Mary were interested. She would hold onto the data. She had certainly learned the value of keeping all the data related to a project. It had proved to be a time-saver in this case.

The entire group reconvened to complete the team ranking on the Cause Analysis Matrix. Using the tool description in Appendix B, pages 175 and 176, they all felt that the catering operation was the greatest contributor to the problem, followed by using the truck for Takeout deliveries.

Cause Analysis Matrix

Cause	We have the resources/power to address the cause directly			Our customer is involved/ impacted*		Individual Ranking	Consensus Generated Team Rank
	Yes	Somewhat	No	Yes	No		
1. Catering Priority Operation	X			X		12212	1
2. Truck Deliveries		X		X		21121	2
3. Tighter Bldg. Access Regulations			X	X		55345	5
4. Illegible Orders	X			X		43453	4
5. Lack of Prep & Set-up Guidelines for Take-Out & Catering	X			X		34534	3

The team decided they were ready to meet with Mary and Jan. They had the causes identified and the data to support them. Tim asked if the group shouldn't have some solutions in mind. What if Jan and Mary asked for ideas on how to address these causes. The group had frequently slipped into discussing potential solutions as they identified root causes. Michael agreed. He'd had a boss once who always said, "If you bring me a problem, be prepared to offer a solution." Tina added that it was always difficult to get Mary and Jan together. So if the team got the go-ahead to keep working, this would be an excellent opportunity to gather solution criteria. They could be more focused on getting this data if they had considered some solutions beforehand. Mae remarked that after all this work, she'd like to have input into the solution, rather than having one she didn't like forced on her.

Thus it was decided to use the first hour of the next meeting to generate some potential solutions and the second to prepare the presentation. Everyone agreed to read Step 5 before the meeting and to bring at least four potential solutions (one per sticky note) to offer. Michael said he'd schedule the meeting with Mary and Jan for the day after. Mae led the process check. Everyone cracked up. She asked them, "If this team were a car, what kind of car would it be and why." At the end of 10 minutes, they had an autographed Mustang drawn on the board. They decided to include it in their presentation. (*To be continued on page 101.*)

Step Five

Creating the Best Solution

GOAL: *Generate and critique all potential actions before committing to a plan. Design and implement a plan to solve the problem.*

Getting started	Preparing the problem and the group	Interviewing the customer	Analyzing	**Creating the best solution**	Implementing the best plan	Monitoring results

Generate Promising Solutions

Select the Best Solution(s)

Develop an Implementation Plan

Develop Measures to Monitor Progress

GENERATE PROMISING SOLUTIONS

Once you have prioritized the causes your team identified as the root of your problem, you are ready to begin developing a solution. This means you will want to know what options are available, how well they meet your customer's and your criteria, and what are the constraints and risks associated with each. After reviewing (discussing) all the information you have gathered about various causes, use the Affinity Diagram process (Appendix A, page 148) to develop a number of potential solutions.

Spend a few minutes individually writing out your thoughts about potential solutions to the problem. As you record your ideas

FIGURE 5–1
Thinking Boxes

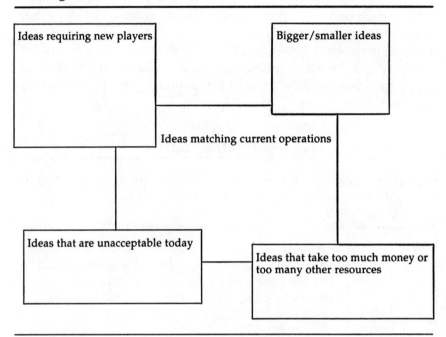

on sticky notes, some questions you might ask yourself about each idea:

- "Does this idea focus on eliminating all or most of the root causes identified (80-20 rule)?
- Am I considering the customer and others who might be impacted by the solution?
- Am I moving outside my box as I think of potential solutions?

Check again the techniques suggested for creative thinking that were presented in Appendix A, page 150.

You want to be sure that you don't stay in your box as you think of solutions. Figure 5–1 can help you expand your thinking. You should be freewheeling—don't worry about constraints associated with any idea at this point in the process. Your goal is to be able to place ideas in each of the boxes. Hopefully many of them will represent solutions you would not consider to be standard-operating-procedures for your organization.

Once each person on the team has had a chance to jot down his or her ideas independently, the group is ready to quickly round-robin all ideas onto flip-charts. During this portion of the process you may ask for clarification, but no discussion, of ideas. Add additional ideas as they come to mind—build off of each other's contributions.

SELECT THE BEST SOLUTION

Choosing a best solution means making an educated guess as to what will resolve the problem and *acting* upon it.

Trap:	Thinking that there is only *one best* solution. Not being willing to take action until exhaustive research has been done, so the team feels they have considered every possible solution and selected the *one best* of all possible.
Solution:	Recognizing that there are generally several solutions that can be implemented in any given situation to solve the problem. The important issue is that the group take action and that all believe the solution will improve conditions. The self-fulfilling prophecy will influence the effectiveness of the path chosen. Waiting too long can negatively impact a situation, just as acting without doing adequate research can.

Once all potential solutions have been generated, your task will be to identify the most viable solutions—ones that the group can explore in greater depth. To do this in an analytical way, use one of the tools discussed in Appendix B. Before you analyze viable solutions, you must determine and categorize the criteria that *must* be satisfied by the solution. These are things that your environment (business and human) dictate be met by a good solution. Make a list of all the data you will need to evaluate if your solutions are viable. Consider elements such as: time, money, customer acceptance, technology, and so on. It is critical to identify your customers' criteria. What will make the solution acceptable to them? You may have to collect more data at this point.

Once you have determined your constraints and customer criteria, you are ready to select the viable solutions through the use of a solution screening process. You want to use a systematic method that is more business-oriented than intuitive to cull through all the potential solutions your group generated in brainstorming and now must reduce to a manageable number of viable options. A matrix helps you determine whether your solutions will meet your requirements. A solution either does or does not meet a criterion. Criteria are those things that must be met. (Examples: Solution can cost no more than $1,000. Solution must be implemented in less than three months.)

Your focus in this step is to find a solution(s) that will improve the process and resolve your problem, while meeting specific criteria and parameters that you may not be able to modify or control. Instructions for constructing the matrix are found in Appendix B, page 189.

Solution Filtering Matrix

Filtering Questions	Solution A	Solution B	Solution C	Solution D	Solution E
How well will this solution meet the customer's criteria?*					
Criteria:					
How well will this solution meet our organization's criteria?*					
Criteria:					
What is the risk to the overall business of implementing this solution?**					
Total***					

* 5 = None or little
  1 = Definitely meet

** 5 = High risk
  1 = no risk

*** Low score is most desirable.

Once you have prioritized your solutions, your team will need to verify that the solutions are achievable in your current environment and have a distinct cost/benefit. In today's workplace of faster, better, cheaper, the cost/benefit of any solution is critical. Your team must focus on this aspect of the solution and be prepared to make your case to those who will be paying the bill for implementing your solution (Appendix B, page 184).

If your solution does not have a positive dollar cost/benefit, your team will need to determine if there are nonmonetary benefits that are important enough to justify this as a high-ranking potential solution to the problem. Sometimes a solution will make it better to do the work. This type of solution may not have a direct impact on dollars but an indirect impact on people who, feeling good about their work, will be more productive. If you can't identify direct dollar benefits, understand that management will not be as receptive to the proposed action.

Another check you will need to make is with the customer. Are your solutions likely to have some type of impact on your customers? If this is the case, and it generally is, you will need to touch base to see how they rank the solutions you have identified. In fact, do they consider the solutions you have focused on to be viable? From their perspective, will the solutions solve the problem as they see it? You may choose at this point to go out to your customers again (you should have done customer data collection during the cause determination phase) to find out how they rank your potential solutions. Or, you may choose to make some internal assumptions about their probable ranking. The option you choose depends on the problem, its importance, and your tie to your customers.

As you do your final ranking of solutions, don't forget the Pareto principle. Will each proposed solution address a major portion of the problem's cause? If you select the right course of action, the cause you choose to address should provide approximately 80 percent of the solution.

If your team is unable to reach consensus or you can't fill in all the blanks, you probably need to spend some time reevaluating. Have you even included the best solution to the problem in your list of options? If you are struggling, some questions you might consider:

- Do we have the right people on our team?
- Have we removed our blinders enough to see a broad range of potential causes and solutions to our problem?

- Have we addressed our process? Are we listening to all group members?

The matrix below can help you double check your list of solutions to be sure that your solution rankings are optimal. It is quite possible that the discussion that surrounds this matrix will cause the team to reassess its ranking of solutions.

Solution Verification/Review Matrix (Appendix B, page 190)

Solution	We have the resources/power to implement the solution		The solution has a positive dollar cost/benefit		The customer is directly interested in the solution		Affirmation of rankings—consensus generated team rank
	Yes	No	Yes	No	Yes	No	

DEVELOP AN IMPLEMENTATION PLAN

Once your team has agreed on the best solution to your problem, you are ready to begin planning for action. The first step in the action process is to *plan* for what you think needs to be done in order to implement the solution. WHO will do WHAT, WHEN, HOW will it be done, and HOW you will know it has been completed.

Trap:	A team selecting a solution and immediately beginning to act without a plan. This results in wasted energy because the efforts are scattered and frequently headed down the wrong path.
Solution:	Use a structured project management approach. This means spending some time up front to plan what needs to be done—who will need to take what action at what phase of the solution implementation, and what checks will be put in place to see that planned-for actions are taken.

Since team members bring a unique set of skills to the team, take some time to have each person individually think through, from his or her perspective, what needs to be done to implement the solution. The team needs to spend some time generating ideas about the actions that need to be taken. Think first in broad categories—what needs to be done in each phase of the project.

The next step is to focus on defining specific actions that will be required, sequencing the events, and assigning tasks. Some groups think forward—we are here and these are the steps to get us to our final point. Other groups think in reverse—here is where we want to end up and this is the sequence of steps backward that lead to the present. Both techniques work, so use the one that is most comfortable for your team.

You will want to create a time line—a continuum on which you can place all activities. Once you have identified your sequence of events, you can begin to flesh out your planned actions with more detail. Try looking at the events from different directions. Consider writing all your action steps on sticky notes. You can then create a time line on a large sheet of butcher paper (4 feet by 6 feet) or on a white board and then mount your events onto the sheet. The sticky notes make it very easy to adjust your sequence as you plan during the initial phase of solution implementation and later as you refine the plan. The fact that you are making it easy to manipulate your sequence of events reinforces the idea that sequences can change.

A continuum guide is shown below. Consider the milestone points that are suggested; use them if they are appropriate to your solution plan. If not, change them based on your needs.

Project Continuum

Start				*End*
Milestones; *Pre-project*	*Early Project*	*Mid-Project*	*Late Project*	*Finalization*

Actions to be
taken—who,
what and when.

Once the team agrees about what needs to be done, the next step is to assign responsibilities—who will be doing what. It is important to do this before you actually begin implementing your plan. A guide is provided to help you identify and record who will be responsible for the various actions. Think in terms of responsibilities, obstacles, completion dates. The matrix below should be reviewed and updated regularly. Just as the continuum can change as the team gets into the project, it is appropriate to transfer actions from one team member to another as needed. Consider this to be a working document, one that changes over time during the implementation phase.

Action Item Matrix (Appendix C, page 202)

Action Item	Responsible Team Member	Key Potential Obstacle	Complete By Day/Month	Status Report	Comments

The purpose in identifying potential obstacles is to help the team plan ahead. If potential obstacles are identified and thought about early, they can often be mitigated or prevented through planning. Discussing them with the team also helps to develop joint ownership for the project. Completion dates and status updates help the team focus on where they are and where they are going. We generally meet goals we put in writing, and if we don't meet them, we are conscious of why we didn't. The status report and comments provide a log of events that can help the team plan more effectively for dealing with similar problems in the future.

DEVELOP MEASURES TO MONITOR PROGRESS

During and after the execution of your action plan, you will need to monitor your progress—quality and continuous improvement dictate this. Your first concern should be to identify what you need to monitor or measure. Once your team has planned its action to implement the solution, you will need to spend some time brain-storming what can be measured or tracked. Focus on what can help you verify whether the solution made a difference. It is critical to put your customer hat on at this juncture because, ultimately, the quality of your solution is in the eyes of the customer. His or her satisfaction with the solution is your goal.

Knowing what to measure will help you determine how best to collect the required information. Think of your measurements as providing you with a barometric reading of how well your actions are meeting your customers' expectations. The information you gain through your measurements will help you determine whether your actions are helping you improve your information, materials, products, or services.

Measurement provides a descriptive, numerical index of your activity. Without measurement you only have a feeling about how you are doing. Measurement gives you an analytical view of your work.

Your measurement process should be built into your implementation plan. You generally need some type of premeasurement that can be used as a norm against which progress can be compared. It is often appropriate to get measures of what is compared to what you would like to have. The resulting gaps give you information about where process improvement can take place.

Trap:	Not having a baseline or premeasure before implementing your solution. Without a baseline you have no way of truly knowing if your solution was the right one—you need something to compare against.
Solution:	Invest the time and energy that it will take to establish baseline data.

You might consider planning a pilot for your solution. This is especially important on very large or politically sensitive projects—these are the ones on which you need to move slowly or gather data about the proposed plan before it is implemented in totality. A pilot is often a way to get support for a project—people see it working and are more willing to get involved when large-scale implementation is done. Being asked to participate in a pilot can also be considered a form of recognition.

Trap:	Not trying out (piloting) the plan and the associated measures before implementing on a large scale, and therefore not resolving bugs that may be in the plan / system.
Solution:	Include in your development plan some method for piloting your solution. Be sure to account for organizational politics so that you include the right individuals or groups in the pilot.

In order to effectively measure your progress, you must determine which measure to use, when. To do this you will need to:

- List all points at which measurement can be made and then refine the list to include the most logical and viable elements.
- Compile a list of potential measures that can address each of the elements you plan to track.
- Identify how the measures will help you determine a customer's satisfaction.
- Determine which measures will aid in improving the work-flow process. Remember, in a quality environment, you should be measuring *process work flow*, not the performance of individual contributors.
- Select measures that are simple and practical.
- Make sure that all team members understand the measures that the team is using to validate its effectiveness.

Once you have identified the elements you wish to measure, you will need to evaluate potential measures to select those that will best monitor your progress. The guide below will help you compare some key concerns that must be met by any measure the team selects:

Potential Measures Matrix (Appendix B, page 203)

	Will the measure provide information about customer satisfaction? If yes, what?		Will the measure provide information about work flow process? If yes, what?		On a scale of 1-10*, how complex or practical is the measure?		All those who will be using the tool understand the measure?	
Potential Measure	Yes	No	Yes	No	Simple	Practical	Yes	No**

* 1 = Least complex/practical
   10 = Most complex/practical

** If no, plan for some type of training. This can range from on-the-job, cross-training to stand-up classroom training. Be sure that all those who might need the training are included (don't forget the customers).

The appropriateness of a measure is linked to your solution. You might keep something as basic as a checksheet counting how often certain things happen. It is a simple matter to keep count in the prechange environment and then in the postchange state. The information is numerical, gives a picture, and shows the improvement. Another measure might be one of perception—asking the customer or user of the solution how satisfied she or he is with the situation before and after the solution is implemented.

Regardless of the measure, you will have to plan ahead so that you can get your baseline data; otherwise, you won't be able to determine how much progress you made, and you won't have any numbers to support your feelings about the effectiveness of your solution. Today's business managers focus on numbers, dollars— measures of value-added.

Understand this and plan ahead to have the hard data you can expect them to request.

Once you have selected your measure, make sure that everyone understands how to use the tool, and that they use it uniformly. This is important for comparative measures. If you find that not everyone is ready to use the tool, plan for some type of training. This can range from on-the-job cross-training, to stand-up classroom training. Be sure that all those who might need the training are included—don't forget your customers.

Trap:	Not everyone accepts, or agrees with, the measure; therefore, the data that is collected is possibly not accurate. This often occurs when: • Appropriate training has not been provided. • Team members are operating with different agendas.
Solution:	To address *training:* provide information on the measure and training where needed. All individuals who monitor the process must know how to gather and interpret the data accurately and uniformly. To address *agendas:* focus on the group process early in the problem-solving cycle to prevent different agendas from developing. If differences are driven by politics, an open discussion of group dynamics can make it acceptable to talk about what is occurring, so that appropriate measures can be agreed to.

Once the measures have been agreed to, the team must develop accountability for monitoring process to assure that it is carried through.

Trap:	Ending up with no analytical measures of your solution's effectiveness.
Solution:	By planning for follow-up to assure that the measurement process is carried out, you are able to assign responsibility for and get buy-in to the process.

The method you use to track your measurement process does not have to be elaborate. It is, however, best done through group process—everyone on the team is involved in some way, and all contribute to the monitoring plan.

Your monitoring plan will need to include the following information:

- Who will do the monitoring?
- What tool will be used?
- What specifically will be measured?
- How often will this be done?

This data can easily be put into a planning format, as in the Monitoring Plan (Appendix C, page 205) shown below.

Who will do the monitoring?	Tool to be used	What specifically is to be measured? operations/process flow	Monitoring schedule

Be sure to regularly check the schedule column. You may need to include monitoring as a regular agenda item at your team meetings or you may choose to post your plan somewhere so that everyone is cognizant of this step of the problem-solving process. Visibility prevents the team from thinking that the process is over once the initial solution has been put into place.

TIME FOR A PROCESS CHECK!

SCENARIO (continued)—Step 5

Meeting 1

The team began the next meeting looking at page 88, Generate Promising Solutions. Danny, the session leader, had everyone mount their sticky notes and used the Thinking Boxes format (see Figure 5-2) to organize the posted information into related categories.

Next they made a list of all the information they would need to determine if these were potentially viable solutions. It included such things as: money for new truck/additional staff, time to correct problem, space availability and identifying the delivery customer's criteria. Questions were also raised: Would customers accept going to a central point on their floor to pick up food? Did they want personal contact with the delivery person? Would they pay more? Would they accept a more limited menu?

At this point the team stopped. They felt they shouldn't go any farther with the problem solving until after the meeting with Mary and Jan.

The team spent the remainder of its session planning their presentation. Michael had reviewed Appendix E, Preparing Your Presentation—Tips, and had put an outline together based on what he read.

The topical agenda they decided upon:

Tell them what you will tell them:

- The problem statement being addressed.
- The three key causes of the problem.
- How addressing these causes will satisfy the delivery problem and restore revenue to projection.
- Ideas for potential solutions.
- Why this group should work on solutions—highly functioning team, know all the processes.
- Recommendations for next steps.

Tell them—present and discuss:

- Review problem-statement refinement process.
- Cause and effect diagram.
- Cause ranking form—be prepared for Jan, thinking that we are attacking her baby, catering; show how potential solutions could make catering even better as well as improve Takeout.
- Potential solutions categories.

FIGURE 5–2

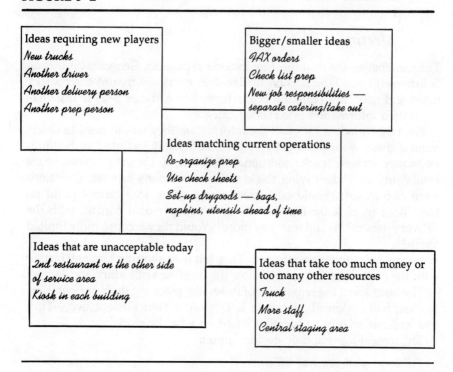

Next steps:

- Recommendation for continuing the problem-solving process.
- Show Mustang—highlight that group is familiar with process and data.
- Get data needed—see constraint/criteria list.
- Introduce next step—plan and timetable.

The team liked the plan. They decided everyone would be involved in the actual presentation. Each selected a section to present. They spent a few minutes anticipating the questions and potential challenges they might get. The group felt they had the data to support their recommendations, and were confident they could present the data in such a way that neither Mary nor Jan would feel challenged. Each team member arranged to practice alone and with each other.

The presentation was scheduled for the following afternoon. It went very well. They got the go-ahead from Mary and Jan.

Meeting 2

At their next session, they reviewed the presentation. Overall they were pleased. As anticipated, they'd had to handle the catering issue with kid gloves, but in the end Jan was giving them lots of suggestions on how it could be improved and was offering to change some things. Danny thought Mary and Jan were being stingy with money. He could understand that maybe they couldn't buy a new truck right now, but it would seem that they could at least spring for a part-time delivery person. Tina stated that although they didn't like all the answers they heard, at least they had a clearer picture of the limitations as well as the opportunities. She suggested that the group revisit their list of solutions and remove any that, based on the criteria heard, were no longer viable. They removed adding a truck and those ideas that added staff.

The team then prepared their Solution Filtering Matrix following the instructions on page 189, Appendix B. There was some discussion about getting more data on customer criteria before beginning. They decided the most critical criteria, hot food hot, on-time delivery, correct order, and so forth, were already known. Other criteria such as delivery person contact could be looked at later if necessary.

Solution Filtering Matrix

Filtering Questions	Solution A Truck/bike	Solution B FAX	Solution C Central Pick-up	Solution D Prep Procedures	Solution E Catering SOP
How well will this solution meet the customer's criteria?*	3	3	3	2	1
Criteria: food temp, on-time, easy ordering, right order, friendly service					
How well will this solution meet our criteria?*	1	2	5	2	4
Criteria: low cost, easy implementation, quick implementation					
What is the risk to the overall business of implementing this solution?**	2	3	4	1	1
Total***	6	8	12	5	6

* 5 = None or little   · 1 = Definitely meet
** 5 = High risk   1 = no risk
*** Low score is most desirable.

As an additional check on the viability of solutions, the team completed a cost benefit analysis described on pages 184–87, Appendix B. The team had worked with Jan and Mary long enough to know that one or both would be asking for the dollar-value impact of their preferred solution.

Cost/Benefit Ratio Evaluation Matrix

VIABLE SOLUTIONS— *Including Associated Resources*	Total Associated Costs	Total Resulting Benefits	Ratio of Benefits to Costs	Expected Payback Duration	Team Ranking of Solutions
Truck/Bike—Staging Area	$200	return to projection	High	Immediate	3
FAX Form—marketing & forms, phone changes	$1,000	Increase business	High	Immediate	1
Central Pick-up—refrigeration, shelving, etc., display cleaning	$3,500	Not sure	Low to mid	1 yr	5
Prep Procedures—more racks, packaging, forms, etc.	$1,500	Increase business	High	6 mo.	2
Catering SOP's—staff hrs to address, forms, more equipment, warming ovens	$2,000	Increase Business	High	6 mo.	4

Although they had all liked the central pick-up solution when they started the process, their cost/benefit analysis showed it as a potentially less desirable solution. They felt they needed more information before they could decide on its status.

Team members still weren't sure if customers would be willing to go to a central pick-up point on their floor or in their building to get their order. Danny said he'd take an informal poll when he did his deliveries the next day. Michael said many companies were not letting delivery people on work floors, so this might end up being a change in the right direction. Danny added that now that there were more restaurants making deliveries, security officers were frequently asking to see access badges. In fact that was one thing slowing him down. Based on this discussion, the team thought that central pick-up would end up with a higher ranking than bicycle delivery. Michael offered to call a few of the building managers to see if a central pick-up area would be permissible and desirable. The next meeting agenda was developed, and the group completed the Team Assessment Instrument. Tina led the discussion. In comparing current results to those of the earlier assessment, they saw that they had higher scores and there was much less variation in response among team members. They were turning into a highly functioning team. Mae said her Bingo buddies were getting tired of hearing her brag about her team! Danny mentioned that he was listening better to his suppliers. In fact he had suggested to the produce guy that they use a fishbone to analyze the wilted lettuce problem. Everyone agreed they were learning a lot from the process.

Meeting 3

The next afternoon after check in, Michael reported that four of the six building managers he'd been able to contact said that they were considering limiting access to major portions of their facilities. All the managers thought a central pick-up point was a good idea.

Danny reported that most of the customers he polled didn't have a major problem with going to a pick-up point as long as it wasn't outside or miles away from their office. Some suggested that a lobby location near the elevators or escalators would be desirable. He noted that they all stated that they hoped they'd still get to see him. Tim chuckled, "Come see Danny between 11:55 and noon and pick up your lunch. If you're late your lunch will be cold and Danny will be gone!" Tina said, "You know, that does bring up a problem. How are we going to ensure that people are on time to pick up their lunches? Danny can't stay at any one place very long or we'll have a bigger problem than we do now."

Michael stated that he was beginning to think that this was a long-term solution that was very viable but that would need a lot of different groups working on it. He was already wondering if some of the other restaurants might want to share the management of pick-up points. He recommended that the group focus on the solutions that they could implement right away. They could recommend that Jan and Mary begin exploring the central pick-up solution. The group agreed.

There was disagreement over the ranking of catering standard operating procedures (SOPs). Many felt it was *the* major cause of the problem. The deciding factor was the amount of control they had in this area. They recognized that change would only come through Jan. They could make recommendations and persuade her with data but that was all they could do. Thus they decided to focus on the prep set-up issues as a beginning point for catering standardization. They completed the Solution Verification Review Matrix in Appendix B, page 190 to determine which solutions to focus on.

Solution Verification/Review Matrix

Solution	We have the resources/power to implement the solution		The solution has a positive dollar cost/benefit		The customer is directly interested in the solution		Affirmation of rankings—consensus generated team rank
	Yes	No	Yes	No	Yes	No	
Bike from truck staging area	X		X			X	2
Central Pick-up in each Bldg.		X	X		X		5
Use FAX Form for Orders	X		X		X		3
Focus on Catering Set-up & Prep	X		X			X	1
Develop SOP's for Catering Service		X		X		X	4

As a result of their analysis, they decided that the three top solutions would eliminate or mitigate 80 percent of the problem.

The team then reviewed Develop an Implementation Plan in Chapter 5 starting on page 93. For each of the top-ranked solutions, the team brainstormed needed action steps, writing them on sticky notes. They followed the project continuum format. They also recognized and noted that the prep streamlining process was going to take the longest time and was probably the most involved. Mae said she'd take responsibility for the food portion of it.

Tim, the leader for the session, suggested they focus on responsibilities by completing as much of the Action Item Matrix (Appendix C, page 202) as they could at this point. Some of the potential obstacles they discussed were: length of time they could leave the catering truck at a staging area, back-up on the fax machine, checking the paper roll on the fax more frequently, getting the fax number to customers and getting them to use a fax for their orders. Tim suggested that they develop a standard fax order form that could be included with each order. Also, Danny could tack one to available bulletin boards when he delivered. They added it to the action items. Another obstacle was staffing to check the catering set-ups. Tina said that using the fax for order taking would free up a lot of her time. Thus she thought she could take over the responsibility for checking all catering setups before they left the restaurant. Danny suggested she might want to create a standard checksheet. At present Jan just scribbled on the catering order form what the setup was to include. In fact he'd noted that most of his emergency runs were to get missing serving utensils, more place settings, and so forth. He'd started stocking extra items on the truck, but space was getting tight as they got more catering assignments. Michael suggested that collecting data on missing catering items and developing a standard checksheet be added as an action item.

They reviewed the completed action plan.

Action Item Matrix

Action Item	Responsible Team Member	Key Potential Obstacle	Complete by Day/Month	Status Report	Comments
Food Prep • Document process • Identify problem points	Mae	Getting input from all the staff	Fri.		
• Develop food Prep and Kitchen guidelines	Tim Mae	Getting input from all the staff	next Wed.		
FAX • Set up process • Design form	Tina	Customer acceptance Collection of orders Maintenance of machine	Process by Wed. Form by Fri.		
• Identify associated costs	Danny	None	Wed.		
• Marketing Material	Michael	Cost Printer response time	next Wed.		
Bike/Truck Delivery • Set up truck & bike	Danny	Parking Delivery time on needed equipment	next Fri.		
• ID best parking spots	Danny	No spots in desired location	Fri.		
• Gain Bldg. mgt. permission if necessary	Michael	Getting "no" from Bldg. mgt.	next Wed.		

Tim announced that it was time to wrap up. The group did a quick process check and then discussed the next steps. They decided they needed a meeting the next day to identify performance measures, focus on how to implement their plan successfully, and plan a presentation for Jan and Mary. After that, they'd meet weekly to monitor the implementation and deal with any hiccups. The team decided that, according to their time schedule, they should wrap up the project with a team debrief three weeks from today. All were to review the section—Develop Measures to Monitor Progress, starting on page 95 before the meeting.

Meeting 4

They started their next meeting by reviewing their action plan. Everybody was still comfortable with it. Next, Mae, the session leader, had them brainstorm potential performance measures, while Danny, the scribe, recorded data on the flip-chart. Using dot voting, they narrowed the list to those the group thought were most critical. They decided the problem wasn't complex enough to complete the Potential Measures Matrix, but they did discuss the questions and complete the monitoring plan presented in Appendix C.

Flip-Chart—Agreed-on Measures

Agreed to measures:
- *Revenue to forecast*
- *Revenue above forecast*
- *Decrease in phone orders of 25% first month*
  50% 2nd month
  75% 3rd month
  with a reverse increase in FAX orders—25% 1st month
  50% 2nd month
  75% 3rd month
- *6 week customer satisfaction check—*
  will ask same question that were originally asked
  Compare data—target: 75% decrease in issues identified
- *Staff morale—6 week check*
  same as 3 months ago
  Better—how much better, why?
- *Track on check sheet—*
  Orders late according to internal time line
  special prep due to order mix-up
  missing items, etc.

Monitoring Plan

Who will do the monitoring?	Tool to be used	What specifically is to be measured? operations/process flow	Monitoring schedule
Tina	Check sheet	• Forms collected from FAX on time • Forms signed off by each area-hot prep, cold prep, set up • Original forms included with order with a personal thanks • New form in bag	1 order checked every 15 min. compared weekly
Michael	Survey questions	• Customer satisfaction	6 wks out
Tim	Focus group	• Staff morale	6 wks out
Danny	Check sheet	• Item delivered within 5 min. of target	Daily, summarize weekly
Mae	Check sheet	• Prep process flow	done before implementation
Michael	Financial reports	• Revenue increase	weekly
Tina	Tally sheets Scatter diagrams	• Usage of new FAX system	daily tally, monthly summary

(To be continued on page 115.)

Step Six
Implementing the Plan

GOAL: *Obtain commitment from key parties for actions that have been clearly defined.*

| Getting started | Preparing the problem and the group | Interviewing the customer | Analyzing | Creating the best solution | Implementing the best plan | Monitoring results |

Gain Organizational/Personal Commitment

Plan for Marketing Your Solution

Execute the Plan and Prepare for the Future

GAIN ORGANIZATIONAL/ PERSONAL COMMITMENT

Before seeking organizational commitment, be clear about who your critical stakeholders are. Spend some time discussing who these individuals are and strategizing how to assure that you can gain their support. The projects and solutions most likely to succeed are the ones that have the active support of all stakeholders.

Some of the information you will need to gather and manage is included in the stakeholder matrix that follows.

Stakeholder Matrix (Appendix C, page 204)

Stakeholder	What kind of commitment is needed describe		Who is responsible for gaining/ monitoring commitment	How will you know when you have the needed commitment	What kind of follow-up will need to be done	Schedule
	Active	Passive				
Internal						
External						

Develop a link between what you want from these individuals and some way of knowing that you have it. "Support" and "commitment" can be very nebulous words. Be clear about what they look like for your team; otherwise, the group can have different perceptions about the support issues, and this may well impact the support you actually receive.

PLAN FOR MARKETING YOUR SOLUTION

You will probably need to make some sort of presentation (formal or informal) to your manager and to your stakeholders. It is important that you develop your marketing plan beforehand. This means thinking through:

- Who you have to market to—what's in it for them.
- When to make your presentation so that it is timely.
- How to make the presentation so that it has the greatest impact on getting stakeholders to buy in and support your solution.

You must have the support of those in the organization who will be impacted by the solution. This is true even if you have the power to implement the solution your team feels is best. You may have the power to make the change, but others are impacted by what you do. Their support is more likely when you spend time strategizing a plan to gain their support. To do this you will need to:

Determine the WIIFM's—you have already identified your stakeholders and thought through what you need from them. Now put on their hat and decide what it is you can offer each individual to make it worth his or her while to support your solution. Each of us has a need to know *what's in it for me* so your task is to think like the stakeholder and identify what you must market in order for the individual to provide the support you need.

Recognize that timing is everything. If you have done your WIIFM work carefully, the timing of your presentation should be easy to gauge. In any organization there are good and bad times to approach a person for support. If you select a good time, your marketing case will be better heard. In planning for your marketing presentation, consider each of the following:

Objective. You should be able to state your purpose in 25 words or less. If you can't do this, spend some time rethinking what you are trying to sell. You might be fuzzy in your goal and this will translate into a loose format that will make it harder to gain support for your ideas.

Agenda. No interaction with customers or stakeholders should occur without a written agenda. See Appendix C for a sample agenda planner. Including time frames should help you retain control of the session. The sequence of the interaction for reaching your solution should follow a logical plan. Remember to constantly wear the hat of your audience—plan the content and structure to match their style. Focus on what they need and want to hear, not on your wants and needs.

Prepare for the interaction. Marketing presentations are best when they are brief and to the point. Most people appreciate content that is well thought out as demonstrated by brevity that doesn't eliminate important elements. Brevity and importance are in the eyes of the beholder—you must do your research around your audience *before* you make your presentation. Knowing what they need to hear rather than what you want to say will determine the success of your efforts.

Handouts. These are generally a plus. They can be the driver of the presentation—what you talk from, or, they can provide supplementary information that participants can read at their convenience (these are generally given as a take-away at the end of the session). Since the material that you give out reflects you and your solution, be sure it is perfect in content and format and that it looks professional.

Participation. Who should do the marketing? Think in terms of presenters as well as attendees. Can one presentation market to all stakeholders? Will you have to do separate sessions tailored to different needs? Should different presentations be done by different individuals within the problem-solving team? These are some considerations your team must evaluate and address if you are to successfully market your ideas. There is no one formula for effective marketing; each problem will drive its own plan.

Environment. Having an appropriate location in which to talk with your customer or stakeholder. Focus on finding a space where you will not be interrupted and where individuals will feel comfortable. Avoid using someone's office unless you can redirect phone calls, shut the door, and have enough room to spread out. Also, remember office space represents *turf* and this can make a difference in the receptivity of the audience—generally a neutral location is best.

EXECUTE THE PLAN AND PREPARE FOR THE FUTURE

Once your stakeholders have heard your plan, agreed with it, and are willing to provide the kind of support you need, you are ready to begin implementation. At this point, you have detailed plans and you have the monitoring mechanisms in place to see that you stay on target.

An additional step is to develop some method for recording thoughts you have during the execution process about making it better next time. This can refer to topic, scope, problems, stakeholders, team members—in other words, you need to think laterally about applying the lessons you learn from the execution of this particular solution. The "ahas" and other thoughts you have are the basis for making the process better and for focusing on continuous improvement—critical aspects of quality.

The format you use to record your thoughts can be quite free form. Keep a notebook, sheets of paper, a log, 3×5 index cards, file folder of snip-its—the critical point is to capture ideas as immediately after the thought occurs to you as possible. These should be unfiltered thoughts—if you think too long before you write your ideas, you will massage them to fit the paradigm you are operating in, and this will limit future improvement. After the project is complete, the team can come together to share ideas.

TIME FOR A PROCESS CHECK!

SCENARIO (*continued*)—*Step Six*

Meeting 1

The team knew the importance of getting support for their plans both inside and outside the organization, so they began the next session by identifying their stakeholders. They used the Stakeholder Matrix (Appendix C, page 204) to assist them in their discussion.

Stakeholder Matrix

	Stakeholder	What kind of commitment is needed— describe		Who is responsible for gaining/ monitoring commitment	How will you know when you have the needed commitment	What kind of follow-up will need to be done	Schedule
		Active	Passive				
Internal	Jan	X		Tina	Makes improvements to catering process	Continually show how catering is benefiting	Monthly update
	Mary	X		Michael	Budget Collecting data for monitoring	Sharing work flow improvements	Monthly update
	Wait Staff	X		Mae	Offer suggestions Automatically use check sheets	Recognition of their involvement	Daily staff meetings
	Kitchen Staff	X		Tim	Offer suggestions Automatically use check sheets	Recognition of their involvement	Daily Staff meetings
	Danny	X		Jan & Mary	His continual involvement	Involve him in on-going review mtgs, recognition	Monthly update
External	Bldg. Mgrs.		X	Michael	Provide data on future plans	Check with them quarterly	Quarterly
	Security	X		Danny	Don't hassle delivery process Provide help Give information	Recognize assistance	Monthly Whenever special effort made

Basically the team decided that Jan and Mary were the key stakeholders. Mae said they might want to consider the wait staff as stakeholders since they were involved in the prep process. Tim added the kitchen crew. They also recognized that many of them were stakeholders in the process, especially Danny. He would have the most to lose personally if it didn't work well. The only outside stakeholders they could identify were building managers and security personnel. They felt that as long as they kept them informed and honored their policies and procedures, they would be cooperative.

The team, as a whole, developed a WIIFM list for Jan and Mary. Tim, Mae, and Tina developed a WIIFM list for the wait and kitchen staff, while Michael and Danny did one for the building personnel. Playfully they did a WIIFM for Danny.

Jan & Mary's WIIFM	Wait & Kitchen Staff's WIIFM
• Increased revenue • Documented procedures • Outline of job duties • Easy to use job aids • Pilot TQM project for Small Business Award and Grant • Project to submit for Entrepreneurial Woman Award • New marketing tool—FAX form • More relevant data basis for decision making	• Less stress • Know when and what expected • Better job aids • Easier to complete tasks • Less hassle from mgt. • Not get in each other's way

Danny's WIIFM	_Building Personnel's WIIFM_
• _Training for triathlon—bike, drive, run_ • _Well-developed/Pecs from biking_ • _Less hassle_ • _More time to visit with redhead at real estate office_	• _Better sense of knowing what's going on_ • _Easier to monitor who is coming into the building_ • _Opportunity to get forgotten food_

It was decided that the entire team would meet with Jan and Mary and that they would divide up to share the plan with the other groups they had developed the WIIFMs for. Since they were running short of time, Tina and Tim agreed to put the presentation together for Jan and Mary. Michael offered to prepare drafts of the simple monitoring check-sheets the team was suggesting. He would also follow up with the printer he'd talked to about developing a marketing flyer for the fax service. Danny agreed to get some figures together on the cost associated with increased fax usage and on some of the other aids that had been mentioned to help streamline the processes involved. Mae said she'd start laying the groundwork with the wait staff.

The presentation to Jan and Mary went very well. They agreed to support the implementation plan and authorized up to $1,500 for the purchase and/or development of any materials. However, they stated that they had to see results immediately. They asked how soon Danny planned on using the bicycle system and when the fax orders were going to start. They also wanted to know who was going to be assigned responsibility for collecting the faxed orders. They were afraid they'd get forgotten in the storeroom. Tina announced that she had added it to her job duties since she already took the phone orders. Michael announced that he had talked with the owner of the quick print shop around the corner, a frequent customer, to see if he'd help design and lay out a marketing flyer for the new fax service. He'd volunteered to design them free and print at cost if the restaurant would cater his Christmas party at cost. Mary and Jan thought this was an excellent idea and told him to get started right away. Mae announced that the wait staff had some ideas for speeding up prep. She planned to test them over the next week. Michael had joined Danny on a run to determine where they could park the truck for up to 30 minutes. They identified five potential spots.

After Jan and Mae left, the team used a "whip" for a process check, simply going around the table and answering the question: What are you feeling right now about our problem-solving efforts? Everyone felt pleased with the process and was looking forward to closure of the process. Solving a problem in addition to doing a regular job was exhilarating, but very tiring.

Meeting 2

At the end of the week, the team got together to see how their plan was coming. Danny said he was making most of his deliveries on time. He shared the tally sheet he was keeping. The biggest problems he'd experienced were having to return to the kitchen for a pair of candlesticks and a security guard who was hassling him about the truck being at the loading dock for 30 minutes. He was told it was OK if he was servicing their building, but not if he was going to others. Michael said he'd call the building manager and see if he could get authorization to park there.

Michael announced that he and Tina had met with the printer and that the marketing piece and the fax form would be ready for distribution on Monday. He reviewed the flyer and its distribution plan. Mae suggested that each sit-down customer be given a flyer with the check. She said that a majority of the sit-down customers were frequent takeout customers, too.

Tim and Mae reviewed the procedures they were developing with the wait and kitchen staffs. Most were on board, but a few were grumbling. Michael suggested they meet with Jan to see if she could help in getting them to be more accepting of the changes. Tina shared the checksheet she had put together for catering set-up. Danny added a couple of things to it. Jan planned on testing it during the next Catering function.

Michael announced that weekly takeout sales had leveled off the last two weeks, but it might have more to do with the cold weather than with the few improvements made to date.

They decided things were on track. Next week would be a big week. They had some catering events and the fax service would be announced. They needed to stay on top of things.

Meetings 3 and 4

The group had two more review meetings. They had survived the crisis week and were seeing the fax service beginning to pay off. Tina was amazed at how much more time she had. She'd never realized how much time was spent taking and writing down orders over the phone. Tim said he really liked it because it was easy to check off as he bagged orders. He jokingly told Mae he wanted her to use the fax form because it would be easier to decipher than her scribbled orders. He also complimented her on the prep work the wait staff was doing. He felt things were better organized and the set ups fresher. It was making his crunch time a lot easier to handle.

Danny said he was getting a crew of volunteer helpers—the security guards. Once they understood the time constraints he was operating under, they called elevators for him, helped to unload the orders, and so on. He felt he had some pretty good relationships going and suggested that the restaurant periodically give the guards something to thank them for all their help. A note was posted on the Thank You chart. The team recognized that they still had a way to go in getting Jan to give them more information about the catering assignments, but they were seeing progress.

Michael announced the best news of all. Revenues for the last week were up 8 percent above forecast. There was a big cheer. The team knew they were on track! Since they were feeling good, they thought it would be a good time to quickly go through their personal notes about what they were seeing and their ideas for improvement. A short round-robin sharing of ideas produced the following flip-chart, which the group intended to reference when they worked on process-improvement recommendations.

Things we observed during execution—
- Need more racks & order dividers in prep and kitchen area
- Fax machine may need to be moved to front
- Need holders for fax forms in all prep areas and next to phone & cashier station
- Shelving and storage areas on truck need to be rearranged by service area—additional shelving needed
- Did not think through as well as we could have on the "hows"— how organize to ensure solution is implemented smoothly
- Need to clearly identify "micro" barriers, internal set-ups, shelving, access to supplies, phone, etc.

(To be continued on page 131.)

Step Seven
Monitoring Results

GOAL: Your problem solution solves the problem and leads to customer satisfaction and continuous improvement.

Getting started	Preparing the problem and the group	Interviewing the customer	Analyzing	Creating the best solution	Implementing the best plan	**Monitoring results**

Plan for a Postmortem

Plan for Follow-Up

Plan for Continuous Improvement

Future Think

Final Process Check

Communicate Results

Say Thank You

Congratulations!

PLAN FOR A POSTMORTEM

After implementing and initial monitoring are completed, the team needs to spend some time analyzing the project—how did the "process" go? Each person on the team should have been collecting data during the execution phase, so you will have as many perceptions of how it went as you have team members. Notice that the operative word is *process*. This focuses on how the team went about its business not on how happy the group was with the solution, the content portion.

Trap:	Only gathering information about results from team members and forgetting to query other stakeholders, and especially the customer, to learn about the process.
Solution:	Part of the process debriefing can include a meeting with stakeholders and key customers. It is also important to determine how they felt about the process used to achieve the solution. If a meeting won't work in your environment, at least send out some type of follow-up instrument or have individual team members make contact with key people by phone or electronic mail.

After the group has had a discussion that includes input from all involved parties, summarize the outcome of the discussion. If appropriate make the contents of this discussion available. To make the information readily available, you should put your observations and suggestions in writing. A quick way of doing this is to generate flip-charts during your discussion, which are kept for future reference. Or you might write a report to your key stakeholders (especially your own management) discussing what you have learned and what you would recommend for future teams.

PLAN FOR FOLLOW-UP

Just because the problem has been solved does not mean you can now forget about the solution that has been implemented. Your team will need to plan for follow-up. In a quality environment, checking back is as important as implementing the initial change.

Some points you need to consider in planning your follow-up process:

- Who will follow up?
- What process will be followed up on?
- What key points will you be checking back on—what will you be specifically looking for in terms of change, maintenance, etc.?
- When and how often will the follow-up be done?
- If this was a spontaneous group brought together to solve a problem, how will all members be kept informed of ongoing progress?

The reason some well-designed solutions are not successful can be traced back to the fact that no one took ownership of the solution once it was reached or progress wasn't shared widely. Therefore, only a few people benefited from the solution. Assume an attitude that says: If the problem was important enough to warrant a problem-solving team being formed, the solution is important enough to be shared.

PLAN FOR CONTINUOUS IMPROVEMENT

Much of the value of problem solving rests in the lessons learned being shared throughout the organization—that is *creating an organization that learns from its own experiences.* Assess:

- What did your team learn (individually and collectively)?
- What things would you do differently the next time?
- Are there lessons or information you want to remember to pass on to others facing similar problem situations?

You might consider holding a brainstorming session to get all ideas on the table. Think in terms of two broad categories:

- Lessons we learned.
- Information we will pass on to others.

Once you have determined what you learned through your solution and its implementation, think of others to whom you might pass on the information. Identify other groups to which your members belong: customers, stakeholders, teams, individuals charged with solving similar problem situations. Make a list and then develop some simple, commonly shared mechanism for getting out information to these groups about problem situations and solutions. Think corporately—all should be able to tap into a common resource that identifies problems, their solutions, and the lessons learned. This will prevent the proverbial reinventing of the wheel.

FUTURE THINK

Solving a problem may mean the end of the problem or it may not. At some point in your finalization process, be sure to have each member of the group answer the two questions below:

1. Is your solution complete? With this action plan implemented, your problem has been resolved and won't come back again.
2. Have potential new problems been identified that will have to be watched for?

Discuss your answers—there should be unanimity.

Remember that quality means continuous improvement. As you make changes to work process, you can expect to create the need for further improvement because new problems will emerge. The team needs to spend some time discussing any probable emerging problems. These are things that will need to be addressed either now (if they have already escalated to new problems) or perhaps in the future (this will mean monitoring a particular situation so that a team can address it when the need arises).

One point to remember: The emerging problems you identify are not necessarily ones you will or should be charged with addressing. The organizational culture needs to be open to problem identification coming from all directions. As you identify emerging problems based on your problem-solving efforts, decide who the logical person is to be informed of the issue. Then see that someone on the team takes responsibility for ensuring that your lessons are shared with the identified individual. If you choose to write a letter or create some type of reference resource around problems and their resolution, you will probably want to include a section on emerging problems.

Organizations need to think of problem identification as a gift—only when we know about something can we take action. Learning about the potential for trouble before it happens can keep your organization competitive.

Emerging Problems Worksheet (Appendix C, page 206)

Emerging Problem	Who on our team knows most about this and will take the responsibility for sharing the information?	Who is the logical person(s) to share our knowledge with?	What exactly will be shared?	By when will this be done?	Backup plan—to assure that something is done with the information we share

Collecting information such as that requested in the matrix above will help your team and organization assume a learning orientation—being sure that experiences of one group become the lessons learned by succeeding teams.

TIME FOR A PROCESS CHECK!

You have moved through a problem-solving process that focused on *content*—what you were solving, as well as *process*—how you went about resolution. At this point your team needs to spend some time discussing how each member feels about the problem-solving experience.

Trap:	Team members not being comfortable in sharing their honest feelings about the problem-solving process. Simply taking a middle-of-the-road stand on the team process survey, and/or not sharing feelings during the discussion process.
Solution:	If your team is not comfortable with open sharing of feelings about the process, adopt some means of precollecting the information anonymously so the group discussion can be conducted at a *nothing personal* level. (This means that answers can be put on the table and no one has to own the response. Thus the group can talk about what was said without associating it with any particular member.)

The final process-check tool found in Appendix C, page 207 and presented below covers some major issues you need to review. In addition, your team can add questions from Appendix C, page 200 that are appropriate to your particular unit's experience.

FINAL PROCESS CHECK

| Our team identified the best possible solution to our problem. | Our team did not identify a good solution to our problem. |

|____6 ____5 ____4 ____3 ____2 ____1 ____|

| Our team appropriately solved our problem. | Our team did not appropriately solve our problem. |

|____6 ____5 ____4 ____3 ____2 ____1 ____|

| Each person on the team was appreciated and listened to. | Not all people on the team were appreciated or listened to. |

|____6 ____5 ____4 ____3 ____2 ____1 ____|

| Communication was supportive and open. | Communication was closed and unsupportive. |

|____6 ____5 ____4 ____3 ____2 ____1 ____|

| Our team addressed process issues as well as content issues. | Our team only addressed issues related to content. |

|____6 ____5 ____4 ____3 ____2 ____1 ____|

Each member is to complete the above statements individually (this can mean reporting responses on anonymous sheets that are collected and discussed blind). The group then needs to talk through team responses. Focus of the discussion is: What can we carry forward to our next problem-solving experience?

COMMUNICATE RESULTS

Once your team has completely solved its problem, a step critical to continuous improvement is the creation of a plan to share your results with other areas.

You might write a report to your key stakeholders (especially your own management) discussing what you learned and what you would recommend for future teams. Letters are to be short and can be effective tools to share results and gain visibility and support for the future. A sample template for such a letter is shown below.

Dear————————,

We have just finished our problem-solving effort around (*insert the issue and/or problem statement here*).

Some major accomplishments that resulted from this effort for our team, organization, and customer are as follows:

(*Insert information about accomplishments here. Be sure to include specific information about how the person you are writing to benefits from your activity.*)

Below are some key points that we learned from our endeavor that we would like to pass on to others who might address similar problems.

(*Insert key learnings—what you learned, how you might do it differently in the future, who could use this information.*)

We thank you for your support during the process and for giving us the opportunity to solve this problem. We feel our results have added value to our organization.

Sincerely,

Trap:	Going through the problem-solving process and then not sharing the learning or results with other units.
Solution:	At a corporate level if possible, agree to share results of all problem-solving teams with the organization at large. Some potential methods for doing this might be: • Hard-copy reports issued by each group at the end of the process. • A common data base in which all results and learning are stored. • Periodic sharing sessions—a time to seek information about whether others have addressed a particular problem. • A repository for all reports, with a summary sheet about each problem-solving team and its outcomes. • Information about groups published in a company wide media resource.

If management is not supportive of this sharing process (but at the same time not vocally against sharing), you might, as a team, independently design some way to let others know about your successes—it may start a grass roots initiative for more sharing.

SAY THANK YOU

Don't forget to say thank you to the people who helped you throughout the problem-solving process. A critical issue in thanking people is to be sure that you recognize them for their effort in an appropriate and timely manner. Thanking someone for something they personally do not value or saying your thank you long after the problem is solved can hurt more than help your future relationship with the individual.

Thank-yous don't have to be elaborate—things as simple as letters, public recognition, or a handshake can be most appropriate. When you compile your list of people, be sure that you remember everyone. Some questions to consider:

Who will you thank? To assure that you thank all involved people in an appropriate and timely manner, have the team spend some time reviewing who helped the process. Consider all categories of support—customers, stakeholders, key resource people. Begin your list early in the process—add names of people as the help is given. If your process is lengthy, it can be hard to remember those who contributed early on. Bring up the issue of recognition regularly in team sessions.

Who on the team should most logically thank the person? Having the right person say thank you is actually a form of subtle recognition, so pick your presenters carefully.

What will you be specifically recognizing? When you give your recognition, you want it to be focused—it means more to a person to know specifically what was appreciated, and it helps them replicate the behavior in the future. "Thank you, Mary, for all your help" is not nearly as meaningful as, "Thank you, Mary, for being sure that we received the XYZ reports within 24 hours of requesting them from you. Getting that information in a timely manner allowed us to maintain a careful watch on our progress."

When will the recognition be given? Timeliness is important. It may be appropriate to recognize contributions periodically throughout an extended problem-solving process. Giving less or smaller immediately is better than waiting to give really big recognition at a too-late date.

What will be given? Personalize when possible. People appreciate your making the effort to think of the *right* recognition for them.

Getting answers to the above questions will help assure that your recognition achieves its purpose, which is to reward those who helped and to encourage them and others to get involved in the future.

CONGRATULATIONS!

You have completed your problem solving using a quality process—from identifying a problem, to determining the critical cause(s), to action planning, to measuring your progress and success, and finally to planning for the continuous improvement of your work process. It is now time to CELEBRATE!!!!!!

Have fun with this. If your team can't immediately decide how it wants to celebrate, apply some of the techniques you have learned throughout this process. Your goal is to select a way to celebrate your accomplishments that pleases the entire team. DON'T WAIT TO CELEBRATE—YOU HAVE EARNED THE CELEBRATION!

As you plan your celebration (some groups are not comfortable with spontaneous celebration), think in terms of:

- What does each member want to do? Find common ground.
- What actions are needed to make it happen? Identify things you need to do, support you will need from management or others (allocation of dollars and time, to name a few).
- When can we celebrate? Decide on and commit to a date— be sure that all participate. To get this participation, the *what you do* will have to have be agreed to by group consensus.

This may seem fairly structured and the antithesis of what celebration should be. However, we have found that many groups have never experienced a celebration at the end of a project, so they either don't know how to celebrate or are uncomfortable doing so. If your team knows how to celebrate, bypass all the above information and simply get together for some fun to recognize all your hard work and your accomplishments in solving your problem.

SCENARIO (*continued*)—*Step Seven*

The next meeting was to be their last. It would be dedicated to looking at how to ensure that the processes became part of the overall operations and to reflecting on their working as a team. They decided that following the meeting they'd all go out to dinner to celebrate.

Last Meeting

At this last meeting, they reviewed their successes and identified a number of things that had helped them be successful. They entered these ideas on a flip-chart, planning to keep the chart so they could use it for their next problem-solving opportunity. Because names were written down, the team decided that they didn't want to post the chart or share it openly with others although they would talk about the information:

How it went—Our postimplementation thoughts—
- *Went very well*
- *Customers commented on Danny's timeliness*
- *They really liked new order form, especially getting a new one with each delivery*
- *Some are ordering a day ahead—new form makes this happen*
- *Many still aren't using fax, but when calling in are giving order in fax format—Tina keeps a supply next to phone*
- *Security guards are becoming very helpful*
- *Jan's decision on the "fly" caused some hiccups, but usually able to stick to schedule*

Tina had done some reading about quality and continuous improvement outside of work. She found the concept personally interesting, so she didn't mind going to the library to read a few current articles or to check out a book. Because of her reading, she suggested that the group think in terms of continuous improvement—how can what we learned help us and others at the restaurant in the future. The team agreed to spend a little time thinking about the lessons they had learned and what they wanted to pass on to others. They came up with ideas that they entered onto two flip-charts, which they planned to mount in the conference room for everyone to see:

Lessons we learned
1. Pay attention to micro business
2. Talk to everyone
3. Always remember who your customer is
4. Data can really help in making decision
5. Don't jump into action— prepare a plan and follow it:

Information for others:
All of the lessons we learned, plus
1. Take time to clearly define your problem
2. Involve others in the process & keep them informed (example:— increased support from bldg. mgt. and security guards after they understood problem and were asked for suggestions)
3. Keep staff informed of progress—many are covering for you—they need to feel that they too have contributed

Next, using the Emerging Problems Worksheet, Appendix C, page 206 they identified the emerging problems. They felt that everyone at the restaurant was aware of the results of their project as they'd all been included in some aspect of the problem-solving process, but they weren't going to assume anything. They listed all the staff by name and then divided up the list so that each team member would personally touch base with staff about the process, tell about how everything turned out, and ask about perceptions people had about the process. This information could be used by future problem-solving groups. Also the fax order form was a process for informing customers. However, they decided that they definitely needed to thank a number of individuals and groups (see page 135).

Emerging Problems Worksheet

Emerging Problem	Who on our team knows most about this and will take the responsibility for sharing the information?	Who is the logical person(s) to share our knowledge with?	What exactly will be shared?	By when will this be done?	Backup plan—to assure that something is done with the information we share
Access Issues	Michael	Mary	Summary of mtgs. with Bldg. mgt.	End of month	Share on-going information collected from Security Guards and Bldg. Mgt.
Ordering by FAX—eating at restaurant	Tina	Mary	Trend starting to note. Speeds up process for customers, but issue of seating and staffing.	After 6 wks of data	Provide trend data for next 3 mo.
Limited parking	Danny	Michael	No. of spots removed in last 6 months—look for any trend	End of month	Explore central pick-up point.
Prep issues—not enough budget to purchase racks that would help in organization	Tina and Mae	Jan & Mary	Impact of make-do situations	Next week	Suggest equipment, alternatives, sliding scale purchasing

Jan and Mary arrived halfway through the meeting and surprised them with a little recognition event. Each team member was given a mug with the person's name on and a T shirt that said: *The FAX Team:*

F-Fast
A-Action
X-eXceptional

The flip-charts generated at the final meeting are shown below:

Flip-charts:

On-going monitoring analysis responsibility:	*Those to Thank* • *Our peers for covering for us while we were in meetings—2 hours off with pay.* • *Security guards—coupon for a free meal (do this periodically)* • *Building facilities offices— a large basket of breakfast rolls or cookies and a Thank You letter* • *Printer—a basket of goodies for his quick response*

It was time to go to dinner. The team decided that they would spend some time over hors d'oeuvres going through the final process check. Basically, they felt good about the process and the resulting improved business operations. However, they now also understood about continuous improvement and knew this meant they couldn't sit on their laurels. More opportunities for improvement and problem solving could be expected down the road.

Concluding the Process
The Learning Transfer

The team has disbanded and it's back to work as usual. But is it? What have you learned that you can transfer to your daily activities and interaction? One of the biggest weaknesses that we've observed in total quality and continuous improvement initiatives is the lack of focus on applying the problem-solving tools to daily operation. There seems to be a sense that we only use them when a team has been formally appointed to address a special problem or issue.

Our contention is that *every* unit is a team whether it is a functional, matrix, project, or informal group. The Team-Based Problem Solver process and the related tools and techniques can be used in any setting. In addition they can be applied individually as well as collectively. What's to keep you from asking yourself as you sit at your desk if you've clearly defined the problem or from drawing a flowchart of the situation? Possibly you'll dial up your E-Mail or the Internet and throw out an idea for brainstorming. We know people who have received valuable input from all corners of the globe and from individuals they did not know. An associate tells of sending out a message that was responded to by someone in their 80s as well as by an 11-year-old. Think of the perspectives that could provide for your issue!

Being a **Team-Based Problem Solver** means that at any time, with any issue, with any associate, you are contributing to the quality of work life by applying these tools and techniques. The following worksheet (Appendix F, page 223) may assist you in transferring your learning to your daily environment. Complete the worksheet after you complete each problem-solving initiative. Then refer to the worksheet periodically to make sure that you continue to grow in your problem-solving skills.

A WORKSHEET FOR
LEARNING TRANSFERENCE

List the team problem-solver skills that you'll be bringing to your daily work environment:

_____

_____

_____

_____

_____

Identify three work opportunities for applying the seven-step problem-solving process.

_____

_____

_____

Who can help you in addressing these areas? What specifically do you need from each person?

_____

_____

_____

What problem-solving tools do you want to standardize in your workplace?

_____

_____

_____

What will you have to do to ensure that they become part of your
work environment?

_____

_____

_____

List three things that you learned about yourself by going through
a team-based problem-solving experience:

_____

_____

_____

How will you use this knowledge to ensure that you are an effective
TEAM PROBLEM SOLVER?

_____

_____

_____

We hope that you will use this new-found knowledge of yourself,
your teammates, and the seven-step problem-solving process to
improve your organization as well as your daily interactions and
individual performance. The *Team-Based Problem Solver* is both a
guide and a resource. Its continual use and the application of this
team-based problem-solving process will enhance your organization's performance and increase your personal competitive advantage.

Hone your skills, embrace change, and **BE** a Team-Based Problem
Solver!

Appendix A

Problem-Solving Tools to Help You Expand Your Range of Ideas

Brainstorming

5 Ws and H

Storyboarding

Affinity Diagram

Nominal Group Technique

Creative Thinking Techniques

Cause-and-Effect Diagrams (Fishbone)

Mapping Technique

Process Flow Chart

Data-Collection Methods for Surveying

Focus Groups

The following tools are fairly simple, and therefore, frequently used in the problem-solving process. If you need more sophisticated tools, you can reference SPC (Statistical Process Control) materials or some of the quality and process handbooks. All of the tools outlined below require minimal materials and training and are suited to self-directed work units who are working through the team-based problem-solving model.

BRAINSTORMING

You will probably use this tool most often during your problem-solving efforts. The technique is designed to help you generate a large number of ideas in a relatively short time. It is dependent on the entire group being able to let go of its need to be correct in exchange for an attitude of high output and creativity. The tool encourages members to build off each other's ideas and to contribute ideas they might normally keep to themselves, feeling that others would not consider their ideas *good enough.*

Times when you might want to use brainstorming in the problem-solving process are:

- To generate lists of potential causes, potential solutions, impacted people, supporting activities, data sources.
- To control the contribution of members—prevents a situation in which a few members dominate idea generation.
- To encourage silent team members to contribute ideas.
- To generate lateral or creative ideas—gets the group to look at a situation differently than they traditionally have.

The brainstorming process needs to be quick and focused—your goal is to get as many ideas out on the table in as short a time as possible. The focus is on quantity not quality—critiquing comes later. To set up a brainstorming activity:

1. Appoint a facilitator. Someone to control the flow of conversation to be sure that all are heard and that no one person dominates. The facilitator must accept all ideas even the off-the-wall ones with an openness that encourages others to think freely.

2. Appoint a scribe. Someone to capture key ideas shared during the session. This person is responsible for writing down everything (not worrying about spelling, grammar, editing for perfection).

3. Determine the specific topic around which the group will be brainstorming. Take time to be sure that everyone is clear on the topic. What is it we are working on? It helps to write the topic onto the top of the first page of the flip-chart page you are using to record the group's ideas.

4. Determine if thinking time is needed. Depending on the group you are working with, consider allowing a few minutes before the actual brainstorming for people to write down their ideas on the topic at hand. Many people are more comfortable sharing ideas after they have had a few minutes to think about what they want to say. There is also a comfort level in being sure you have something to say and in knowing how to say it because it is written out. If you aren't sure about allowing this time (will people want it or consider it a waste of their time), ask the group how they want to proceed—with or without the thinking time. Or, simply try it both ways during the problem-solving cycle.

5. Decide on a time limit for the session. Brainstorming periods—if purely idea-generating sessions—are usually short, no more than 10–15 minutes.

6. Establish guidelines. If this is a new group, take the time to establish your guides; if it is an ongoing group, review them. A sample set of Brainstorming Guidelines is shown below:

Brainstorming Session—Guidelines

- Focus on quantity—generate as many ideas as possible within the timeframe—keep the energy up.
- Creativity is important—building on others' ideas is not only permissible, it is desirable.
- Consciously include ideas that counter tradition, that are in left-field, that we *can't do here.*
- Criticism and evaluation of ideas is not permitted—you can, however, ask for honest explanation or clarification after the initial brainstorming is completed.
- Record all ideas on a flip-chart or board. If you must condense ideas, have the contributor come up with the *shorthand* statement.
- Only one idea is added to the list at a time—if ideas flow quickly in the group, have multiple scribes.
- Move freely among ideas—there is no correct starting point or sequence for idea generation.
- All ideas are good ones—avoid self-criticism or filtering of what is said.

7. Decide on the type of brainstorming to use.   There are two basic approaches to soliciting team-member ideas: An *around-the-table approach* in which each member is asked to share one idea. The facilitator moves around the table calling on each person in turn. The group continues offering ideas in an orderly manner until no one has anything else to add. A danger with this approach is that you stifle some ideas because of the adherence to structure. A plus is that all members will share their ideas. A *spontaneous approach* in which members call out their ideas spontaneously. Idea contribution continues at will until no one has anything else to add. The challenge in this approach is to be sure that everyone in the group contributes—there is a tendency for quiet people to get lost. The facilitator must be very skilled in watching nonverbals and tracking contribution and in pulling ideas out of those who have made no, or minimal, contribution. There are usually people in any group who have excellent ideas, but who feel no compulsion to share them unless asked. An advantage of this format is that there is greater spontaneity, which can result in greater creativity.

8. End on time. The power of brainstorming is in its machine-gun approach to getting lots of ideas out quickly, so don't let the process drag. Obviously, if you have just started a binge of ideas, you may ask the team if they wish to extend the time period.

5 Ws AND H

I kept six, honest serving men.
They taught me all I knew.
Their names are What
And Why and When
And Where and How and Who.
                    Rudyard Kipling

This is a very simple questioning technique for helping the team make sure it has addressed each of the six question categories implied in the name:

Who

Determines who is involved in the problem. You need a 360° view to be sure you include all stakeholders—team, customer, management, suppliers, and so on.

What

Focuses on what is. It includes knowing the problem, the potential causes and solutions, and the processes involved in the problem, to name a few factors. Questions the team can ask: What are we doing? What do we need to know about this?

When

The time-focus issue. It looks at time-related issues around the problem, as well as the timing of the implementation process. A sample of time factors: When does the problem occur? When do we have to be done? When will the solution be used?

Where

The physical locations, as well as process issues. The question can be, Where? meaning which location has the problem. It can also mean, At what point in the cycle does this occur?

Why

Seeks to determine cause. Why is something happening? Why are people reacting? These questions generally require probing.

Use some caution in using "why" questions. These can be perceived as interrogations, and thus can be threatening to the other person. "Why did this . . ." is better than "Why did you . . ."

How

Can reference cause (How did this happen?), or it can look at solution (How can we fix this?).

The team needs to construct its six questions, record them at the top of flip-chart pages, and then spend some time brainstorming answers to each question.

Questioning is a tool that helps you avoid misunderstandings and misinterpretations. The purpose and value of questioning is:

- It keeps the discussion on the problem at hand—keeps stray issues from clouding the real issue.

- It avoids getting into personality issues—effective questions are directed to the issue, not the person.

- It diminishes the possibility of an argument—you are asking for information and clarification, not making direct statements that can sound accusatory.

- It helps focus on factual information rather than assumptions—you are asking and encouraging the other person to rephrase what was heard (explicitly or implicitly) in your statements.

- It clarifies issues that are vague—pulls out detail that might not have been offered originally.

- It encourages finding a solution that is agreeable to both parties—assists in the collaborative problem-solving process.

STORYBOARDING

This is a simple but powerful technique that helps teams gather and process a breadth of ideas in an efficient and effective way. It encourages a team to look at a problem from several perspectives. Some of the key points of the technique:

- It is a quick way to generate many ideas that can be retained and even reused because they are portable.
- It can be used with any type of problem and at many stages of the problem-solving process.
- It aids teams in organizing and sequencing their ideas.
- It is easy to add to or reduce the data being looked at and worked with because it is card driven.
- It is easy to sort collected information.
- It is a technique that requires few supplies and that is easily understood and used.

The steps in the process, which you can vary to meet your team's specific needs, are as follows:

Preparatory

- Provide each team member with an ample supply of index cards (use sticky notes if you prefer)—use different colors and sizes.
- Have enough space available so the cards can be spread out, arranged, and rearranged as you build your *board.*

How to

1. The topic under discussion is clarified and agreed to by all team members—it is then posted for all to see.
2. Each person writes all his or her thoughts related to the topic—one idea per card. (Variations—use different color cards for different idea categories. Use large cards and represent ideas on the left half of the card with pictures; on the right half, use words that express the idea.)
3. Through group discussion, completed cards are sorted and categorized on a "board" (usually a large sheet of butcher

paper, a whiteboard, or a blank wall). Sort into major topical areas related to the problem being explored. Sub-ideas that expand or support the main thought are positioned beneath. The sorted cards graphically display the relationships between topics and the flow of ideas up a category silo.

4. Once sequence is agreed to, narrative, detailed information, or action plans are provided to support each silo of cards.

5. Cards that were withdrawn during the sorting process are assessed. Do they require further/future action? Do they reflect an idea that should be passed on to another work unit?

Use the storyboard whenever you want to develop ideas. It allows the team to produce a great number of ideas, and it provides a flexible tool for rearranging information that can lead to innovative approaches to solving problems.

The Affinity diagram described below is a variation of storyboarding.

AFFINITY DIAGRAM

Use this technique to generate and organize large numbers of ideas into natural groupings that are based on the relationships among the ideas. It can help a team be more creative in its thinking and less businesslike or analytical. The technique encourages participation by all team members and it assists the team in organizing any amount of information quickly. Use the technique at the beginning of the problem-solving process when thinking is still unclear and the group does not yet have a handle on the issues. A value of the technique is its focus on broad-based information, rather than on detailed thinking about specific topics. It encourages paradigm-breaking thinking because it focuses on quantity.

To construct an affinity diagram:

1. Identify the issue to be addressed by the team. Ask, "What are the issues involved in . . .?"

2. Brainstorm ideas around the topic—use index cards or sticky notes to record ideas, one idea per card.

3. Post written ideas in random order. If necessary, spend some time clarifying posted ideas. But note this is not to be a critiquing or discussing session.

4. Sort ideas into topical or related groupings Each person looks at and arranges the posted ideas as he or she sees fit; sorting is done in silence.

- **Some cards will stand alone—don't force relationships.**
- **Intuition should be the driver of idea arrangement—don't allow anyone time for deep, analytical thinking.**

---

5. Capture the essence of each grouping with a header card that identifies the common theme of the idea group. All cards in a group should be reflected by the header—conversely, the header should be able to stand on its own and be meaningful. Remember, stand-alone ideas are okay.

6. Draw lines around each group to finalize the diagram. Notice: Ideas can be part of multiple groupings.

7. Show the diagram to others who might be affected by the problem resolution. Ask for their input and critiquing—add any new ideas that surface.

When you are through, you will have a pictorial representation of all issues and thoughts related to your problem topic. The picture should identify for your team what will need to be addressed next: core problems, root causes, viable solutions, and so on. (See Exhibit A–1.)

NOMINAL GROUP TECHNIQUE

This tool helps assure that everyone on the team has an equal voice in selecting a problem or in providing input around an issue faced by the group. Team members work in the presence of each other but only interact verbally at specified times. The technique emphasizes

EXHIBIT A–1
Affinity Diagram

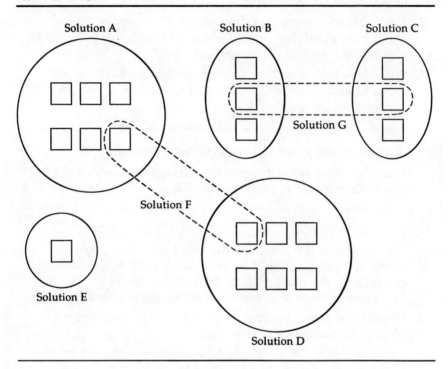

individual contribution and numerical analytical evaluation of the options. Some reasons for selecting the nominal group technique for idea generation might be:

- To counter a strong personality on the team, prevent one person from dominating and unduly influencing the group.
- To prevent *group think* or the *Abalene paradox* from hindering group product. (With both of these phenomena, individuals within a group refrain from expressing a difference of opinion. As a consequence, the group makes a poor decision because insufficient challenges were raised to force the group to carefully assess its proposed action or direction.)
- To improve input provided by a team made up of people from different organizational levels. This is especially useful

when some in the group might be intimidated **by** others
with higher corporate status.

- To draw information out of teams with many *quiet*
members.
- To force the team to look at all options and move away
from the *obviously correct* solution that is driven by current
paradigms and corporate history.

The steps are described below:

1. Each team member, working independently, writes down
the problem or issue that she or he feels is the most
important for the group to address—there is no talking or
sharing of ideas (some groups choose to write ideas onto
sticky notes or index cards—one idea per sheet).
2. The group reconvenes and all member ideas are recorded.
If you initially write ideas on sticky notes or cards, these
can be collected, posted, and read—there is no discussion
at this time.
3. Every posted idea is discussed in order to clarify and
elaborate the data—all ideas are discussed, and none are
eliminated. However duplicate ideas can be consolidated.
4. Each member independently ranks all ideas.

**If you are working with a large number of ideas, you can have
each person rank half the total number of items plus one. This
will allow less viable alternatives to be eliminated.**

---

5. Without discussion, rankings from all team members are
recorded. Numbers are summed. The item with the largest
number is the most important. The team begins work on
this item first, moving on to others as needed. (The Pareto
80/20 rule may result in the first item reducing enough of
the problem that further work isn't warranted.)

The outcome of the process: Information that represents the team's
listing of all potential causes of the problem and identification of
the most likely root causes, which become the basis for the next
step of the problem-solving process.

CREATIVE THINKING TECHNIQUES: HOW TO GET YOURSELF OUT OF THE SAME OLD THINKING BOX

Step back and look at the ideas your team is generating. If they have the flavor of being the *same old stuff*, it is probably time for you to practice a little creative thinking. This requires the team to take some structured action to force itself to think about its problem in a different way—sometimes called lateral thinking. There are many techniques and resources available to foster this type of thinking when you have become boxed in by, The way we do things around here, or, That will never work here, or, They won't let us try that, thinking patterns.

A couple of techniques are described below. If you are interested in exploring other creative-thinking exercises, there are many books and aids to help you with the process. Edward DeBono and Roger von Oech have developed many materials in this arena. (See Bibliography.)

1. *What if we?* This is a questioning process that helps the team to look at its problem from a different perspective. The team poses the question below to itself during idea-generation time. The question is asked several times—each time a different verb drives the question. Some potential question drivers are listed in the box below:

What if we	Reverse Magnify/enlarge Combine two of Minimize/reduce Simplify	our current idea/approach?
	Add others that your team dreams up	

2. *Relating the unrelated*—this technique gets the team to think about something totally unrelated to the topic under discussion.

EXHIBIT A-2
Thinking Boxes

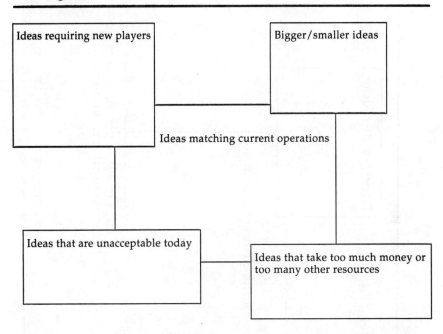

The group brainstorms around the topic (be sure it is off-the-wall) for a short period of time and then goes back to the topic of concern. The goal is to find ways of linking the unrelated items to the problem being discussed.

3. *Fill in the blanks*—use the chart Thinking boxes to help you break out of your thinking box. Your goal is to enter ideas into all of the boxes. (See the fill-in version of Exhibit A-2 on next page.)

CAUSE-AND-EFFECT DIAGRAMS (FISHBONE)

Cause-and-effect diagrams provide a visual representation of the relationship between an effect and its myriad of potential causes. The standard format is to have the effect stated on the right and the probable causes on the left. The lines connecting probable causes and the effect resemble a fish skeleton, thus the name *fishbone* for the process of constructing a cause-and-effect diagram. (See Exhibit A-3.)

EXHIBIT A–2
Thinking Boxes

EXHIBIT A-3

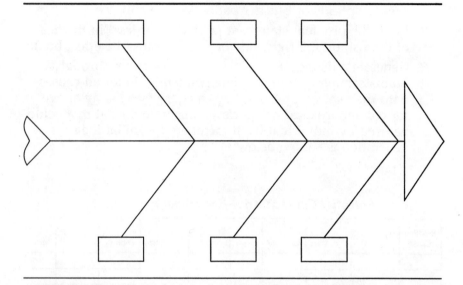

In problem solving, you frequently need to categorize the ideas you generate in order to work with them most efficiently. To help with the grouping process, you might consider the categories listed below, which are fairly generic and fit most business problem situations:

- People.
- Machinery.
- Methods/Systems.
- Material.
- Policies.
- Procedures.
- Physical environment.
- Training.

These are suggestions; you probably won't use all the categories listed. You will need to establish categories that are meaningful to the problem you are addressing. The sequence for developing a cause-and-effect diagram follows:

1. Draw your fish on a sheet of paper that is large enough to allow you to list all causes by category and large enough

for all team members to read easily (a 4 foot by 6 foot
sheet of plastic or butcher paper works well).

2. Enter the problem statement (25 words or less) in the head
   of the fish on the right side of the diagram (the effect box).

3. Generate a listing of all potential causes either through
   brainstorming or working independently. Enter all causes
   onto the fish, group causes by category (see listing above
   for commonly used categories). A sample format that could
   be used by individual team members for initial idea
   generation is shown below:

Potential Cause Matrix—Individual Assessment

Potential Cause	Communi- cation	Procedure	Materials	People	Environ- ment	Equipment	Training	Measure- ment	Misc.

4. Primary causes are entered onto the main "bones" coming
   off the backbone. For each cause ask, "Why does it
   happen?" Answers represent sub-causes which are entered
   as "small bones: branches off the major ideas."

> Causes can be verbally brainstormed, with the scribe recording
> ideas in the proper category. Or individual members can write
> their causes onto sticky notes or index cards that are mounted on
> the appropriate bone on the fish. The advantage of the second
> option is that it gets the group more involved because of the
> activity.

5. Once all causes have been entered, begin a process of
   clarification, condensation, and evaluation of items you
   have listed. Discuss entries, assure that all items listed are
   causes and not symptoms, and determine which causes
   you can address and which need to be referred to another
   body in the organization.

6. Prioritize causes, that is, determine which are the key causes (the 20 percent that will cure 80 percent of the problem) that will become the basis for future action planning. Frequently the cause filtering and multivoting tools described in Appendix B are used to establish priorities or gain focus.

Check the scenario (Step 4 beginning on page 80) for a completed sample of the fishbone. Be sure to draw your fish on a sheet of paper large enough to accommodate the input from all team members.

Potential Cause Matrix—Individual Assessment

Potential Cause									

MAPPING TECHNIQUE

This is a pictorial approach to presenting a broad range of ideas about a topic. It is quite useful in the initial data-gathering stages because it allows for brainstorming and at the same time groups or maps the data as they are generated. When the process is complete, the team has a picture of all the ideas related to a particular issue clustered by key topical areas. In addition relationships among items within one cluster and between different clusters are identified.

To draw a map:

1. Place the key issue in the center of a large sheet of paper.

2. As ideas are brainstormed, place major idea categories on different areas of the sheet, keeping the central issue in the middle of the page.

EXHIBIT A–4

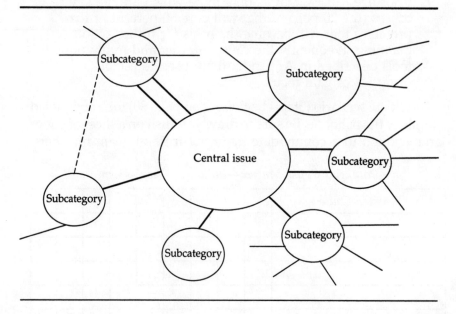

3. New ideas can be entered alone if they represent a
   different category, or they can be clustered around another
   idea that they support.
4. Color can be used to distinguish different idea categories—
   all ideas related to a topic are entered in one color, those
   related to another, are in a different color.
5. Key relationships can be shown by lines that connect
   different clusters. Directional arrows can be used to show
   relationships.

At the end of the process, the team has a quick visual representation
of clustered ideas.

A sample map is shown in Exhibit A–5.

This tool provides a team with a quick, structured approach to
idea generation. Once key ideas have been identified, the team can
select the most promising categories and explore them further,
using tools that probe more deeply.

PROCESS FLOW CHART

This is an easy-to-use tool that allows you to map a process that you have decided to study. It helps you analyze what is transpiring—how is the process currently operating. By using this tool, you can identify steps that can be modified, combined, or eliminated. It provides you with a step-by-step picture of a particular process. Use it when you want to:

- See how your suppliers or customers fit into a particular business process.
- Determine exactly who does what in a business process.
- Gain a pictorial view of where the problem is in a process.

Trap:	Using the tool before you have determined which processes should be examined.
Solution:	Spend time assessing the value-added of your processes—does it make a difference to the customer? Charting takes time, which equates to dollars. Be sure you are retaining those processes that are important to the customer. Once you have identified these, you can begin to chart as a first step to improvement.

Charts can range from a simple series of rectangular boxes, each representing a major step in the process you are analyzing, to a complex multipage analysis detailing a process through many layers of substeps. The traditional symbols used for charting are shown in Exhibit A–5.

At its simplest, the flow chart in Exhibit A–6 demonstrates how to chart a macro process:

This type of high-level flow of a process can be detailed:

- The process can be assessed to determine if it is important in the eyes of the customer.

EXHIBIT A–5

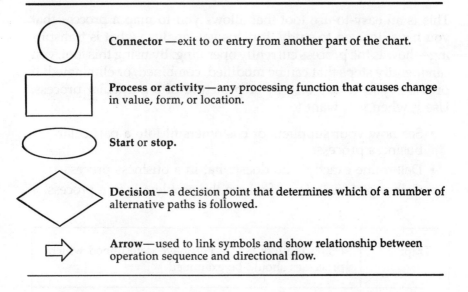

Connector —exit to or entry from another part of the chart.

Process or activity—any processing function that causes change in value, form, or location.

Start or **stop**.

Decision—a decision point that determines which of a number of alternative paths is followed.

Arrow—used to link symbols and show relationship between operation sequence and directional flow.

- The high-level steps can be evaluated to determine if they add value to the overall process.
- Specific steps in the process can be studied and improved.
- Work flow can be studied—how does the process flow through the workplace? Who is involved in the process and should they be? Is there excessive delay or idle time? (Idle time can account for as much as 90 percent of total cycle time.)

The goal of the analysis is to first determine whether the process should be done and then to look for ways to improve it.

EXHIBIT A–6

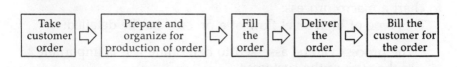

| Take customer order | Prepare and organize for production of order | Fill the order | Deliver the order | Bill the customer for the order |

DATA-COLLECTION METHODS FOR SURVEYING

Data-Collection Planning*

You need to think in terms of the method you use for collecting your data (the **how**), and you also need to think in terms of the sources of that data (the **what**). Some questions to ask:

1. What data do we need to collect?
2. How should we go about collecting the data?
3. What format will give us the most useful information?
4. Who should collect the data?
5. How is the team going to analyze the data?

The following example lists were developed for identifying employee skills deficiencies. They provide you with some ideas to consider as you plan for your own data collection:

The HOW:

Questionnaires

Work participation

Surveys

Direct observation

Assessments

Statistical analysis

Interviews—In-Person/Telephone

Checklists

Testing

Inventories

---

* A data collection form can be found later in this Appendix. See Scenario (Step 3, page 65) for a completed sheet.

The WHAT:

Evaluations—Peer / Customer / Management

Management input

Job descriptions

Individual development plans

Human resource plans

Survey of needs

Assessment center data

Knowledge test data

Advisory committee input

Attitude surveying data

Performance appraisal

Skill inventories

Performance objectives

Focus groups

Skills tests data

Historical data

Psychological instruments

Exit interviews

Task analyses

Surveying Options

Data collection surveys will help you gather information on critical customer issues that you want to measure and compare. They are useful in identifying problems, gathering data for problem analysis, and measuring the success of a solution. Surveys may be in a written format or simply gathered from verbal comments made by the customer.

Experiential and environmental elements will influence the particular data-collection method you select. Some key elements you will need to consider when you choose a data-collection method are listed in the left column of the matrix shown below. Determine the element, then, based on your experience, the amount of data needed, the resources available, and so forth. Select a method from one of the three right-hand columns. For example: If you were considering the sensitivity of data and you had a lot of experience, you would choose in-person interviews—the right-most column.

Element under Consideration	Little	Some	A Great Deal
Your experience in using data collection methods	• Historical data • Structured interviews	• Mail questionnaire • Card questionnaire	• Direct observation • Unstructured interviews
Time available for collection	• Mail questionnaire • Historical data	• Group interviews	• Direct observation • Unstructured interviews
Experience/sophistication of the people being contacted	• Historical data • Structured interviews • Mail questionnaire	• Card questionnaire • Group interview	• Unstructured interview • Direct observation
Number of people included in the process	• Direct observation • Unstructured interviews	• Card questionnaire • Structured interview	• Mail questionnaire • Historical data
Geographic spread among people being contacted or between you and audience	• Direct observation • In-person interview	• Phone interview	• Mail questionnaire • Historical data
Money available for process	• Historical data • Mail questionnaire	• Phone interview	• Direct observation • In-person interview
Amount of data you can commit to collecting	• Direct observation • Unstructured interviews	• Card questionnaire	• Mail questionnaire • Structured interviews
Sensitivity of data	• Mail questionnaire • Group interviews	• Card questionnaire • Structured interview	• In-person interview

Developing Survey Questions

To gather your data, you will need to design effective and unbiased surveying questions, ones that will allow you to gather data to clarify critical customer issues in a way that frees the information from your preconceived assumptions.

The following are some guidelines for you to consider as you develop your team's questions:

Use rating scales. These are especially useful when they contain an even number because they force respondents to make a positive/negative choice by eliminating the neutral middle option.

Force comparison. Instead of asking if something is acceptable, yes or no, ask respondents how one thing compares with another.

Ask open-ended questions. These are questions that encourage comment. Although you have less control with this type of question, you are much more likely to gain valuable input (understand that some may not be directly related to the current problem but should be kept for future reference).

Test your questions. Use a pilot or focus group to assure that your questions will be understood in the same way by all respondents and that they are unbiased. Be sure that the phrasing does not suggest what the desired response should be.

Share results. After you have analyzed the data, summarize results and offer to distribute them to those who provided you with input.

Data Collection Form

	Checksheet													

														TOTAL
TOTAL														

FOCUS GROUPS

This is a technique that helps you gather in-depth information on a specific topic by interviewing groups of people who share a common experience or base of information. The outcome of the meeting is data that reflect the attitudes, feelings, and perceptions of attendees around the topic being discussed. It allows you to glean a lot of subtleties and detail about the subject, based on the nonverbal input provided in addition to content information offered by participants.

Use focus groups when you need to make qualitative decisions around a topic about which you have no objective data. The basic premise behind the technique is that if you must make a subjective decision, the views and judgments of many people are better than those of one.

Some points to consider when planning for and conducting such a group:

- Optimum size is 8–10 participants.
- Allow 1-1/2 to 2 hours for a session.
- Seek homogeneous grouping around any given topic—use several groups if you have subgroups within your population. For example, don't mix managers with their subordinates.
- Questions are important, so keep questions open ended and targeted to the topic and audience.
- Select a skilled facilitator for the session—this person is pivotal in influencing the success of the session.
- Plan for a structured method of participation, use a scribe. Taping can be used if all in the group agree.
- Determine some method for distributing results of the session.

When handled properly the focus group helps you generate candid information about your topic. You will generally get feedback that is concrete enough to provide direction for future action.

The cost per participant can make this an expensive technique, especially if travel is involved. Some questions that can help you decide whether or not to use this tool:

1. Given the kind of information you need to gather, will a focus group provide relevant information (that is, are you looking for qualitative data that you can't learn about through other means)?
2. When do you need the information? Focus groups take time to set up and to run. Data generated takes longer to analyze.
3. Will the information gathered be used? Don't ask people to provide input if you will not apply their suggestions in a visible way.
4. How important is the topic? Does it warrant the cost of this technique?
5. Do you have the resources available to manage the focus-group process?

Some situations in which a focus group might be warranted:

- Analyzing performance.
- Evaluating specific projects.
- Trouble-shooting a proposed program or change.
- Evaluating impact of pilot program or ongoing change effort.
- Assessing customer needs and satisfaction.

Analysis Tools To Help You Gain Focus On Solutions

Problem-Solving Readiness Survey

Customer Requirements Matrix

Pareto Charts

Consensus

Cause Analysis Tools

Multivoting

Ranking/Voting Techniques

Criteria Matching

Scatter Diagram

Cost/Benefit Analysis

Gap Analysis

Solution Filtering Matrix

Solution Verification/Review Matrix

The tools in this appendix are designed to help you reach decision points or key milestones. You will use them after you have spent time exploring potential options and when you have a broad understanding of what will probably be needed to improve a situation (what you learned by using the tools in Appendix A). They will also help you get a handle on an unwieldy number of options.

PROBLEM-SOLVING READINESS SURVEY

The table below provides an explanation of why each question in the readiness survey is important. A duplicate copy of the survey is included at the end of this section.

Item No.	Survey Question	Rationale
1.	Is your team **ready** and **able** to act on the issue you have identified?	Unless you are actively ready to get in and solve the problem, there is little justification for calling a problem-solving team together. **Ready** includes things like having the people and systems in place to support what you are doing. It also means that at a personal level—emotional and positional—team members are willing to take on the problem now. **Able** includes resource issues—time, money, equipment, etc.
2.	Is at least one member of your team positioned to have the **power to authorize** any action you may determine to be necessary to solve your problem?	Problem solving only works when you can act on your solutions. This means that the problem-solving team includes or has immediate access to the person with the power to say, "Go/No go." Sometimes the person with decision-making power sets checkpoints and gives the team authority to act within limits. At each checkpoint, the team must check in and get approval for further work. This approach is successful as long as everyone knows who the decision maker is and the checkpoints are clear to all.

Item No.	Survey Question	Rationale
3.	Do you have the **best people** to work on this problem?	Generally the best people are those who work daily with some aspect of the problem and / or are positioned to be involved / concerned as regards outcome. A key to success is to be sure the group has the authority to make decisions and initiate action.
4.	Have you identified / included all **individuals whose input will be required** in the problem-solving process—for the entire project and as interim *subject experts*?	Often there are people whose expertise we seek only after the project is well under way. Poor timing of information gathering can set a project back or result in poor decisions. The team frequently needs to ask itself, Have we forgotten someone? An example is bringing in the information systems function late in the cycle when their input early on might have provided alternative methods the team didn't consider because of lack of knowledge. Not everyone needs to be present for the entire problem-solving cycle. As a need arises for a certain type of expertise, bring in the appropriate person. Sometimes people are appreciative that they are asked to participate only when their expertise is required. At other times, the team and the expert realize that the person should become a permanent team member.
5.	Is there a **system in place** to obtain appropriate sign-off at the various stages of the process?	A system is necessary when the team has the responsibility for problem resolution, but still needs outside-the-group approval in order to proceed. It is also useful on extended projects as a mechanism for keeping the group together and on time. Be sure everyone involved agrees to the system you adopt—procedurally and time-wise.

The team needs to answer each of the questions with a yes response before proceeding. Poll the group question by question. Discuss statements to which any group members answered no. What the group does next will depend on the discussion. Sometimes the no response becomes a qualified yes, meaning the group can proceed as long as certain conditions are met. Sometimes it means that you are not in a position to solve the issue you have come together to address.

PROBLEM-SOLVING READINESS SURVEY

Answer yes or no to each question below:

_____ 1. Is your team ready and able to act on the issue you have identified?

_____ 2. Is at least one member of your team positioned to have the power to authorize any action you may determine to be necessary to solve your problem?

_____ 3. Do you have the best people to work on this problem?

_____ 4. Have you identified and included all individuals whose input will be required in the problem-solving process—for the entire project and as interim subject experts?

_____ 5. Is there a system in place to obtain appropriate signoff at the various stages of the process?

CUSTOMER REQUIREMENTS MATRIX

Use the matrix below to answer the following questions about your customers and their requirements:

1. Who are our customers? (List and then identify as internal or external)

2. What service or product do we provide each one?

3. How important is the customer you've identified to the success of your organization? (Very, Somewhat, None or little)

4. How much would each customer identified benefit from this problem being resolved? (**Very, Somewhat, Not** likely)

Customer Requirements Matrix

Customer	Internal or External	Service/Product Provided	Importance*	Benefit*

* **V** = very important to the organization/beneficial to the customer
  S = of medium importance to the organization/benefit to the customer
  N = none or very minimal importance to the organization/benefit to the customer

PARETO CHARTS

This tool displays the relative importance of data. It is a form of histogram or vertical bar chart—one that prioritizes the importance of the variables you have included in your analysis. It can quickly point to where focus and resources will be needed (tallest bar equals greatest impact as a general rule).

The steps to construct a Pareto chart are:

1. Determine the variables to be measured, and collect data.
2. Sum the data for each variable category.

> An easy way to deal with a number of concerns that have little associated data is to create a Miscellaneous or Other category.

3. Draw the x axis (horizontal) and list the variable categories in order of magnitude—most to least (left to right).
4. Draw the y axis (vertical) at the left side of the horizontal axis, and number it. Start with zero at the intersection with the horizontal axis and end with the sum of all responses for all categories.
5. Draw a bar to represent each variable. The upper limit is the number of total responses for that category.
6. Give the graph a title and put the completion date on it. (See Exhibit B–1.)

> A variation of the Pareto Chart also includes the cumulative percentage of the total for each category above its bar and next to a dot referenced to the right vertical axis which tracts percentage of problem source 0% to 100%. For example, if the first bar is 26% of total complaints and the second is 24% of total complaints, the dot for the second bar will be at the 50% point. Connect the dots—they will reach the 100% mark with the addition of the last variable.

CONSENSUS

Consensus means that every member on the team is at least 70 percent comfortable with the solution at hand and is 100 percent willing to support it. A solution arrived at by consensus is one that everyone accepts because the group has taken the time to talk through all ramifications of the option. It is one that all can accept and support for their own personal reasons.

Reaching consensus means that everyone on the team has a win in the solution—it differs from other methods of choosing because it doesn't create a win/lose relationship among team members (win/lose often results with voting techniques). It represents a higher, more-difficult-to reach plane and can often result in an

EXHIBIT B-1
Sample of Pareto Chart—Customer Complaints

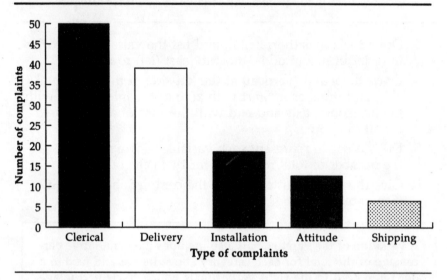

option being accepted that wasn't under consideration when the team began the focusing process. Consensus is reached through talking—the team must allow enough time for all options to be thoroughly discussed and for **every** member of the team to share her or his view.

- Each person is responsible for practicing effective listening skills including nonverbals and active listening.
- Avoid arguing for your view—everyone must have the opportunity to state his or her views and all in the group must *listen* openly to each other.
- Win/lose is not acceptable—the group must work, through discussions, to find the most acceptable alternative that meets the needs of the entire team.
- Confrontation should *not* be avoided—it is expected that members will disagree on options and that they will work through the conflict.
  - ☐ Yield only when you believe another option is superior to the original.

☐ Voting or trading support is not acceptable as a way through conflict.

☐ Predetermine conflict resolution techniques that your group will use.

• Consider using a facilitator to guide the process.

Trap:	Reaching consensus too easily or readily and attributing it to effective team operation.
Solution:	Complete a group process check. Quick resolution may be a warning that members are not being totally honest in expressing or supporting their views.

CAUSE ANALYSIS TOOLS

Cause Filtering

This technique helps a team determine which of the causes it identified through a cause-and-effect process are the most likely root causes of the problem. It can provide the group with a way of determining which causes, if addressed, are most likely to have the greatest impact on solving the problem.

To complete a Cause Filter, follow the steps outlined below:

1. Through discussion, verify that all the causes listed on your cause and effect diagram could result in the problem.

2. As a group identify the likelihood of each cause occurring. Remember the rules of consensus. Use the following categories:

V = Very likely
S = Somewhat likely
N = Not likely

Put the agreed-to category letter next to each cause being
examined. Code all causes before moving to Step 3.

3. Discuss how easy the cause will be to fix. Consider such
conditions as who has to be involved in fixing the cause or
how much time or how many dollars will be necessary.
Sometimes, on the surface a cause appears easy to fix. But
if you don't have control of the situation or resource to
address it, it can be very difficult to fix. For each cause,
determine which of the following categories matches the
cause:

V = Very easy to fix
S = Somewhat easy to fix
N = Not easy to fix

Place the agreed-on code next to the letter from the previous
vote.

**Using two colors, one for likelihood and one for fixability makes
it easy to track input.**

---

4. Evaluate coded causes referencing the following guide:

VV—Consider these causes to have quick payback.

VS—These will most likely result in payback but will
require more energy and resources to implement.

VN—Can result in a permanent fix, but will require greater
expense and redesign.

Decide which cause(s) should be addressed. Discuss all the
V's, considering criticality, timeliness, and risk. Identify
those root causes that will reduce 80 percent of the
problem.

5. Establish an action plan for the selected cause(s) and then
verify the results through testing.

6. Select another cause if the problem still persists. Optimally your first selected cause eliminated 80 percent of the problem. Decide if this expectation was met. If it was, further attention to the problem may not provide enough value-added to warrant continued attention to the problem. If it wasn't, examine why you didn't achieve the desired percentage of improvement, and then select another more appropriate cause (if the team decides that this was the problem).

Before addressing any of your root causes, brainstorm potential solutions. There may be a creative solution that eliminates the need to address causes. Eighty percent of the time, the only way to effectively solve a problem is to chip away at the root causes. However, creative solutions that circumvent the need to address specific causes have been generated and this has eliminated the need for expensive or difficult corrective action.

Example: **Departments that have their budgets cut 30 percent develop better solutions and become more effective units than those that experience a 10 percent cut.**

Cause Analysis Matrix

This tool assists in ranking identified causes. Once the team has determined probable causes for the problem, the next step is to prioritize them and decide which ones are most viable for the group to address. Two determiners of whether a cause can or should be addressed are (1) the ability of the team to do something to correct the cause, and (2) the importance of the cause to the customer.

The Cause Analysis matrix is meant to be a vehicle for team discussion of causes. Once each team member has completed the columns through individual ranking, the group is to discuss responses and then reach consensus about which causes it should explore further.

Cause Analysis Matrix

Cause	We have the resources/power to address the cause directly			Our customer is involved/impacted*		Individual Ranking	Consensus Generated Team Rank
	Yes	Somewhat	No	Yes	No		

* The customer column needs to be considered carefully. A "yes" response in this column indicates that your customer will need to be involved in some way in the problem-solving process if he or she is not already included. A "no" response means that you can move on without customer contact.

If the customer is involved, consider your options:
- Use the information from your customer interviews to rank the causes.
- Make some internal assumptions about their probable ranking.
- Move no further on the problem until the customer can be included in the process. Invite the customer to participate in the problem-solving process.

The option you choose depends upon the problem, its importance, and your tie to your customers.

MULTIVOTING

This tool provides a way to select the most important items from a long list. Multivoting requires a series of votes, each one reducing the list of options by approximately two-thirds. At the same time it provides an opportunity for members to express minority opinions. Consider using this tool after brainstorming, when you are trying to reduce the number of items to be explored further. It reduces discussion time, so consider using it when your problem-solving time is limited.

> Whenever possible, group decisions should be made through discussion and consensus. Techniques like multivoting should be used only when lengthy discussion or consensus is not possible.

The process steps are:

1. Generate a list of items (through brainstorming or some other idea-generation technique).
2. Remove duplicate items and combine similar ones.
3. Team members identify those items they would like to discuss or work on. This is done by placing a colored mark or dot by each person's preferred items. Each member is allowed a number of choices equal to one-third of the total number of items on the list. (Example: With 24 items on the list, each person identifies 8 items; with 60 items, 20 choices.)
4. Remove all items that did not receive any votes.
5. Hold a minority discussion—discuss items that received a minimal number of votes (voted for by less than 20–25 percent of participants). If everyone agrees to removing an item, do so. However, if after discussion the person(s) who originally voted for the item still feels it is very important, it is left on the list for another vote. Only the members who voted for an item can remove it from the list.

Trap:	Not listening to the rationale for the minority vote.
Solution:	The value of team problem solving is the different viewpoints that members bring. Discussion surfaces this information and knowledge and needs to be encouraged. Experience has shown that frequently it is the oddball idea that is the best idea or the catalyst for effective action.

6. Repeat steps two through five with the remaining list, vote, and reduce accordingly. Continue the process until only a few items (generally a maximum of five) remain. If no clear choice is identified by this point, have the group discuss which item(s) should receive top priority, or one last vote can be taken.

Trap:	Not having the patience to follow the steps because they appear to take too long.
Solution:	Although it may seem to be taking a long time, this combination of voting with minority discussion is a much faster process than pure group consensus decision making.

RANKING/VOTING TECHNIQUES

These include a variety of methods a team can use to rank/vote for preferred options and thus reduce a large number into a manageable few. Some techniques you can use:

Dots

Give each team member an agreed-to number of stick-on dots. These are posted next to each individual's preferred options among all those listed through an idea-expansion process.

Generally five to seven dots are given to each team member. The person votes with the dots for those options he or she feels are most viable, important, or critical. How dots are voted can range from a maximum of one dot per option to all dots allocated to a single option or any variation between. The number of options under discussion and the opinion of the team should be considered in setting up the team's rules for voting.

High-Low

Each team member is given a preset number of dots/sticky notes in two different colors. These are used to vote for the top and bottom options. This is a way of segmenting a list of options into important/less important groupings.

Whenever you use a voting mechanism (dots, strips of paper, etc.), consider the number of options being voted on and the number of people in the group. As a general rule, try to reduce your list length by at least two-thirds with every vote.

Verbal/Show-of-Hand Ranking

The team, verbally or through a show of hands, votes for each of the options—this can be a yes/no vote with sums being used to rank the list of items. This technique is usually quicker (a positive) but it is least private (a negative) and can be easily influenced by strong team members.

When using a voting technique, remember that it is not the same as consensus. You are asking your team to reduce a large number of options to few options. Generally you will want to be sure to include a critical option of each team member—you might do a process check after you have identified your options for further analysis. Questions to ask:

1. Is a top option of every person included in the list?
2. Does everyone feel he or she had the opportunity to fully express opinions about the options during the discussion phase so that informed choices could be made by the team during voting?

3. Does anyone feel so uncomfortable with any particular option that he or she feels a need to further discuss that item?

If there is any disharmony, be sure to resolve it before proceeding. The purpose of voting is to take a large number of options and quickly reduce it to a manageable size. This is appropriate as long as everyone is comfortable with the reduced items. If all team members are comfortable, the group is ready to move ahead. Do not use this technique for the final selection process—at this point in the process, it can lead to win/lose feeling among team members. Only use it for preliminary focusing.

CRITERIA MATCHING

This is a technique that allows you to match solution options against a master list of criteria that an acceptable solution must satisfy. The process allows you to separate those options that are viable because they meet your needs and wants from those that do not.

Checklist—this is a very simple form of criteria matching. The team develops a checklist of all the elements that must be present in a solution. Each option is compared to that list—those that satisfy the checklist are kept for further discussion and analysis; those that don't, can be discarded, studied further to see if they can reasonably be modified to meet the list, or referred to others because they represent good ideas that should be considered.

Criteria matrix—this technique highlights elements that *must* be satisfied by any acceptable solution and those that would be desired (*wanted*) but that could be done without if necessary. Assuming you have generated viable solutions, you can expect several options to meet the must category. Among those options, a varying number of wants also will be satisfied. This second category will direct your discussion—which wants are most important and provide the greatest value-added.

To create your criteria matrix:

1. Begin by brainstorming a list of all the criteria that any solution you implement needs to satisfy.

2. Reduce the list to the most important eight to ten criteria through any of the decision-making processes discussed in this appendix.

3. Categorize the criteria as **musts** and **wants** as you enter them in the column at the left:

   ☐ **Must criteria**—ones that must be satisfied by any solution you might consider—without satisfaction, **the** solution will not be acceptable.

   ☐ **Want criteria**—ones that, if satisfied by a solution, make it more desirable. They help you to prioritize the potential solutions—the more wants satisfied by a solution, the better choice it is.

4. The potential solutions you identified earlier are placed along the top of the matrix.

5. Discuss/analyze each potential solution based on the criteria the team established as **must/want.** Identify those solutions that are viable because they satisfy **must** and **want** criteria. (You can use an absolute evaluator such as Y/N or a scaled evaluator such as 1–7 when determining the degree of criteria satisfaction for each potential solution you included in your team list.)

6. Eliminate all solutions that do not meet the **must** criteria. Prioritize the remaining solutions based on how well each satisfies the **want** criteria.

A copy of this form follows.

Criteria Matrix

	Criteria		Solutions					
			A	B	C	D	E	n*
Musts	1							
	2							
	3							
	4							
	n*							
Wants	1							
	2							
	3							
	4							
	n*							
	· Rating Totals							

* Reflects any number of variables that are appropriate to include in the analysis.

SCATTER DIAGRAM

Use the scatter diagram to represent graphically the relationship between two variables. The tool displays what happens to one variable as you change a second one. You are able to determine possible relationships between two variables and show the strength of the relationship.

The diagram is arranged so that the measures for the independent variable are shown along the horizontal (X) axis, and the measures for the dependent variable are shown on the vertical (Y) axis. An example of the scatter diagram is shown in Exhibit B–2.

EXHIBIT B–2
Sample Scatter Diagram

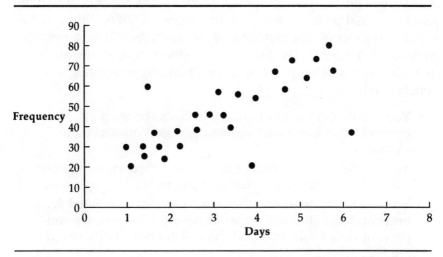

The direction and closeness of the plotted points gives you information about the strength and type of relationship between the elements you are measuring. The more the cluster of points appears to be a straight line, the stronger the linear relationship that exists between the variables. To construct a scatter diagram, you will need to do the following:

- Collect paired samples of data—information about what you think the cause to be and what you think the effect to be.
- Draw your X (cause variable) and Y (effect variable) axes. Label intervals along each axis to accommodate your high and low data values.
- Plot your data on the diagram.

The scatter diagram helps identify patterns. Close linear patterns suggest a strong correlation between your two variables—the tighter the line the greater the relationship. A scattered pattern suggests no relationship exists. It is important to remember that relationships are simply that, they do not necessarily imply causation. A strong relationship suggests that you will need to explore further the tie between the two variables.

COST/BENEFIT ANALYSIS

A cost/benefit analysis compares the costs and benefits of two or more potential problem solutions that were identified through the expansion process. The outcome of the analysis will be a priority ranking of solutions. The team can use the results of the analysis in its decision-making process. Some situations warranting a cost/benefit analysis:

- You are dealing with quantifiable costs/benefits of options—you can easily see and precisely measure the elements.
- You are selecting among options that reflect ongoing costs— things like rental, maintenance agreements, leasing costs.
- You are trying to justify the costs/benefits associated with preventative solutions—if we choose this option, we can prevent this, avoid that and the dollars potentially saved are _____.
- You are dealing with options that are one-time costs—start-up costs, equipment purchase, staff training on new equipment.

Your analysis will help you map out the relative costs and benefits among the viable solutions to your particular problem. You will end up with a dollar and cents statement and a ratio to support the solutions you are recommending. Most decision makers are influenced by hard dollar numbers, so consider including a cost/benefit analysis as part of your marketing plan.

First, determine for each of your viable solution options the costs and the benefits associated with the option. (You can estimate these or gather hard figures depending on available resources, plans, audience for the analysis.) Once you have the data for each of your options, you can compare dollars.

A point to consider: Dollar savings constitute just one element that needs to be considered in the decision-making process. Don't select an option solely on the basis of dollars. As you build your benefits list, consider some of the intangibles that can be critical.

The following Solution Analysis Guide provides a format for the analysis process. Use it to assess each potential solution. (A complete copy of this form is included at the end of this section).

	Associated Costs		Resulting Benefits	
Potential Solution	Item	$	Item	$

If you divide your resulting benefit dollars by the associated cost dollars for each solution, you will have a ratio of benefit to cost:

$$\text{Ratio} = \frac{\text{Benefit}}{\text{Cost}}$$

If you are computing your costs for an annual period, you can divide your ratio into 12 months to determine how long the payback period will be:

$$\text{Payback} = \frac{\text{Months}}{\text{Ratio}}$$

Most senior managers like to see a payback period of one year or less, but check within your organization to determine its expectations. Once you have calculated the ratios for each of your options, you can compare the ratios. Be prepared to present graphically your data to your marketing audience. A sample presentation would include:

Viable Solutions	Total Associated Costs	Total Resulting Benefits	Ratio of Benefits to Costs	Expected Payback Duration	Team Ranking of Solutions

(A copy of the above Cost/Benefit Ratio Matrix is included. Your team needs to be able to explain its ranking of solutions and to show the relationship of ranking to the recommended problem solution. Remember, you may not select your number-one ranking—this is quite acceptable, you just need to be prepared to discuss your selection with your key stakeholders.

Solution Analysis Guide

	Associated Costs		Resulting Benefits	
Potential Solution	Item	$	Item	$

Cost/Benefit Ratio Matrix

Viable Solutions	Total Associated Costs	Total Resulting Benefits	Ratio of Benefits to Costs	Expected Payback Duration	Team Ranking of Solutions

GAP ANALYSIS

Use this technique to assess the difference between what is and what should be in an area where you have decided to take action. This tool can help you set performance expectations. The theory behind gap analysis is that if you know where you are today in any performance area and you have a clear picture of where you need to be based on future expectations for performance, you will be able to develop action plans that will allow you to migrate to the new level of behavior. The key to the success of this analysis process is:

- Clear statements or questions that enable you to establish current performance level and future expectations.
- The information you gather about current expectations from the appropriate individuals—usually customers.

Generally, items are presented with two response columns—
one reflecting today's state and the other establishing expectations
for a future point (usually one to two years into the future).
To conduct the analysis, you will need to:

1. **Develop statements or questions** around the performance
   areas you are interested in. Since the items will determine
   the value of the data, it will be important to pilot your
   survey and to get input into the items from key
   stakeholders.
2. **Decide the future point.** As a general rule, when you ask
   how respondents would like it a year from now, you are
   going to get information that reflects how they wish it
   were today. You will need to determine whether you are
   interested in determining your performance/product gap
   today or in establishing some future expectation goals in
   which case you would choose a point further out than one
   year.
3. **Collect your data.** If you are not familiar with surveying
   processes, check a research methods text for help on how
   to survey effectively.
4. **Analyze your data** to determine gaps and to establish
   which ones are significant and need to be acted upon.
5. **Validate your findings**—numbers don't always tell the full
   story.
6. **Develop action plans** to close the gaps. Be sure to include
   methods to gain buy-in from stakeholders and
   communication links to let those who provided
   information know what you discovered and what you will
   be doing to reach their expectations.

A sample format for a gap analysis is shown at the end of the
section. The gap width information in Column 4 would be the
basis for future action. The gap is determined by determining the
difference between current state and desired state.

Gap Analysis Format

Surveyed Item	Current State	Desired State at x Point in the Future	Gap Width
1.	1 2 3 4 5	1 2 3 4 5	
2.	1 2 3 4 5	1 2 3 4 5	
3.	1 2 3 4 5	1 2 3 4 5	
4.	1 2 3 4 5	1 2 3 4 5	
5.	1 2 3 4 5	1 2 3 4 5	
6.	1 2 3 4 5	1 2 3 4 5	
7.	1 2 3 4 5	1 2 3 4 5	
8.	1 2 3 4 5	1 2 3 4 5	
9.	1 2 3 4 5	1 2 3 4 5	
10.	1 2 3 4 5	1 2 3 4 5	

SOLUTION FILTERING

This technique allows you to evaluate the degree to which your potential solutions will satisfy the following filters:

- Customer criteria.
- Team or organization's criteria.
- Degree of risk to the overall business.

Before using this tool, the team must look at solution criteria from the perspective of both the customer and the organization. Some time must be spent brainstorming criteria and then determining the importance of each item.

See the scenario, Step 5, page 104 for a completed form.

Solution Filtering Matrix

Filtering Questions	Solution A	Solution B	Solution C	Solution D	Solution E
How well will this solution meet the customer's criteria?*					
Criteria:					
How well will this solution meet our organization's criteria?*					
Criteria:					
What is the risk to the overall business of implementing this solution?**					
Total***					

* 5 = None or little
   1 = Definitely meet
** 5 = High risk
   1 = No risk
*** Low score is most desirable

SOLUTION VERIFICATION/REVIEW MATRIX

Use this tool when the team is working with a limited number of solutions that have already been discussed and analyzed from a cost and impact basis. The tool will help focus on the value-added by each potential solution and to reaffirm the team's earlier ranking of potential solutions. Once you have completed the steps of this matrix, your group is ready to act.

A duplicable copy of this form follows.

Solution Verification/Review Matrix

Solution	We Have the Resources/Power to Implement the Solution		The Solution Has a Positive Dollar Cost/Benefit		The Customer Is Directly Interested in the Solution		Affirmation of Rankings—Consensus Generated Team Rank
	Yes	No	Yes	No	Yes	No	

Appendix C

Planning and Monitoring Tools

Our Team Guidelines
Meeting Agenda
Team Leadership Survey
Team Process Check—Short Form
Team Process Check—Long Form
Team Assessment Instrument
Additional Process Meeting Check Questions
Action Item Matrix
Potential Measures Matrix
Stakeholder Matrix
Monitoring Plan
Emerging Problems Worksheet
Final Process Check

Most of the following pages contain the blank forms that you will need to plan and monitor your problem-solving efforts. Each of the forms included in this section has been discussed and demonstrated within the text of the model or in the scenario. The form masters are exhibited here and on the disk. As with all forms in this model, use them as guides. If you wish to modify them to meet specific needs of your particular team, please do so.

OUR TEAM GUIDELINES

As a team, we have decided that these are the guidelines we will follow for all problem-solving sessions. It is the responsibility of each member to apply these guides to his or her behavior.

- _____
  _____
  _____

- _____
  _____
  _____

- _____
  _____
  _____

- _____
  _____
  _____

- _____
  _____
  _____

- _____
  _____
  _____

- _____
  _____
  _____

Agenda

Team: _____   Date: _____
                          Time—start: _____ end: _____
                          Location: _____
Leader: _____   Timekeeper: _____
Facilitator: _____   Scribe: _____
Purpose:

Meeting preparation: Background/Premeeting assignments:

                    Please bring:

Agenda Item	Responsible Person	Process to Address Topic	Time	Expected Outcome	Actual Outcome*

End-of-meeting   Evaluation technique/process: _____
planning: Action to be taken: _____

*To be filled at the next meeting to be sure that there are no unfinished items and to document actions agreed to.

TEAM LEADERSHIP SURVEY—WHAT DOES IT LOOK LIKE FOR US?

In the space provided below, write your responses to the questions. When you are done, discuss your answers with the team. As a group, define the leader and facilitator roles for your team and identify the support responsibilities of the team members. These will then become part of your team guidelines.

1. How do you want these roles performed?

   team leader?   facilitator?

   _____   _____

   _____   _____

   _____   _____

2. What don't you want from your

   leader?   facilitator?

   _____   _____

   _____   _____

   _____   _____

3. How can you effectively support the initiatives and efforts of your team leadership?

   _____

   _____

   _____

TEAM PROCESS CHECK—SHORT FORM

Each team member is to complete the statements below. The team facilitator will then lead a group brainstorming/discussion around each item. Focus on process **not** individuals—the input is about what was happening in the session, not about individual team members.

What did you like most about today's process?

_____

_____

_____

_____

_____

What would you like to have had occur differently—and how?

_____

_____

_____

_____

_____

What would you like more/less of in future sessions?

_____

_____

_____

_____

_____

TEAM PROCESS CHECK—LONG FORM

Each member is to answer the questions below and the team is to discuss responses. Reviewing process allows the team to share perceptions—all perceptions are accurate for the individual providing the view. Focus on listening to input and asking constantly— How can we use what we hear to make our process better than it currently is? Use the comments section to record points you need to remember or wish to act upon.

Group Question Checklist	Yes/No/ Somewhat	Comments
1. Did the meeting follow the planned agenda?	_____	_____
2. Were no more than 10 minutes (if that much) spent on review and warm up activities?	_____	_____
3. Was time used effectively?	_____	_____
4. Was there encouragement to participate— everyone was comfortable sharing their views?	_____	_____
5. Were useful ideas generated?	_____	_____
6. Were people open to ideas of others—did we LISTEN to each other?	_____	_____
7. Did the group attempt to reach consensus on important decisions?	_____	_____
8. Did we follow our Team Guidelines?	_____	_____
9. Are we following the problem-solving steps?	_____	_____
10. Is the team using the problem-solving tools appropriately?	_____	_____
11. Are all team members volunteering for various team roles and action items?	_____	_____
12. Is everyone completing their team assignments—on time and in a quality way?	_____	_____

TEAM ASSESSMENT INSTRUMENT

Circle the number that best reflects your feelings about your team's progress thus far. Fill in the sheet individually then discuss responses with the entire team sharing their feelings.

What I say is listened to with attention/respect.	What I say is ignored or not heard.

|___6 ____5 ____4 ____3 ____2 ____1 ____|

What I say is prized and valued here.	What I say is discounted or belittled.

|___6 ____5 ____4 ____3 ____2 ____1 ____|

I like the way the group is working together as a team.	I have a number of concerns about the group's interaction.

|___6 ____5 ____4 ____3 ____2 ____1 ____|

I am pleased with the progress the group is making in this session(s).	I do not feel the group is on target—we have wasted time being here.

|___6 ____5 ____4 ____3 ____2 ____1 ____|

ADDITIONAL PROCESS CHECK QUESTIONS

You will want to plan for process checks at different times during the problem-solving cycle:

- After ongoing meetings.
- When facing blockages.
- At the end of the process.
- To check on individual effectiveness.

The questions below are grouped according to these different categories. Consider using them for your process checks. Select items that are appropriate for your group—base the selection on the type of check being done and the nature of your team. Use items from one category, or include a cross-section of items (some items are appropriate for more than one category although they are only listed once).

Questions to use for ongoing meeting checks:

1. Did the meeting follow the planned agenda?
2. Did we use our time effectively?
3. Our meetings can be defined as being productive (we meet our objectives for the session and we are progressing toward our problem-solving goal)?
4. Did we make *real* progress in solving our problem?
5. Did we do a good job of exploring options?
6. Did everyone help manage the discussion process—expand when necessary and close when appropriate?
7. We feel informed about what's going on within the problem-solving team?
8. We encourage different team members to take leadership of the group at different times?

Questions to help a team through a blockage:

1. Was there encouragement to participate?
2. Are we following the problem-solving process? If not, where are we slipping?

3. Are we following our own guidelines? If not, which are we breaking?

4. Conflicts are openly discussed and resolved?

5. Do we respect/trust each other?

6. Do we have a team identity—do we all feel as if we belong to this group?

7. Do we understand the necessary team roles and know who plays which role on our team?

8. Can all team members get their ideas across in our sessions, and if we don't understand, are we willing to say so and ask for clarification?

9. Are we clear on who all the stakeholders are?

10. Did we agree up front to the problem-solving approach we are using?

11. Are we practicing effective questioning techniques— nonjudgmental, asking for clarification?

12. Are we open and honest with each other?

13. Have we been able to get to the core problem and root causes?

14. Are we clear on roles—who fills them, how well they are being filled?

15. Do all team members want to be on the team?

Questions to use at the end of the process:

1. Did we follow the guides on reaching consensus—when we needed to, could we use the process to reach agreement?

2. Were we clear about and comfortable with using the various problem-solving tools?

3. Have we done a good job in getting the support we need from our stakeholders?

4. Did the team adopt a useful approach to solving the problem?

5. Did we operate as a team?

6. Did we stay on target throughout the process?

7. Are we committed to what was accomplished by the team?

Questions to check on individual effectiveness:

1. Do team members understand their responsibilities on this problem-solving team? Are all team members willing to assume their fair share of responsibility?

2. Are we open in our communication with each other?

3. Are we balanced in our contributions to team product— although we may not do everything exactly the same, do we all contribute fully to the solution?

4. Do all team members practice active listening, including appropriate nonverbal behavior in meetings?

5. Are we willing to share our feelings in addition to factual information when we are discussing issues related to our problem?

6. Are group members overly nice and polite to each other?

7. Do some team members agree with others too quickly or disagree just for the sake of argument?

8. Do we each take responsibility for expressing our ideas clearly and concisely?

9. Do we each take responsibility for making others feel at ease?

10. Do we recognize our differences and demonstrate flexibility in accepting viewpoints/behaviors of other team members?

11. Do we provide helpful feedback to each other?

Action Item Matrix

Action Item	Responsible Team Member	Key Potential Obstacle	Complete by Day/Month	Status Report	Comments

Potential Measures Matrix

Potential Measure	Will the measure provide information about customer satisfaction? If yes, what?		Will the measure provide information about work flow process? If yes, what?		On a scale of 1–10*, how complex or practical is the measure?			All those who will be using the tool understand the measure?	
	Yes	No	Yes	No	Simple		Practical	Yes	No**

* 1 = Least complex/practical
10 = Most complex/practical

** If no, plan for some type of training. This can range from on-the-job cross-training, to stand-up classroom training. Be sure that all those who might need the training are included (don't forget the customers).

Stakeholder Matrix

Stakeholder	What kind of commitment is needed— describe		Who is responsible for gaining/ monitoring commitment	How will you know when you have the needed commitment	What kind of follow-up will need to be done	Schedule
	Active	Passive				
Internal						
External						

Monitoring Plan

Who will do the monitoring?	Tool to be used	What specifically is to be measured? operations/ process flow	Monitoring Schedule

Emerging Problems Worksheet

Emerging Problem	Who on our team knows most about this and will take the responsibility for sharing the information?	Who is the logical person(s) to share our knowledge with?	What exactly will be shared?	By when will this be done?	Backup plan—to assure that something is done with the information we share

FINAL PROCESS CHECK

How do you feel about this problem-solving experience? Mark the scales below to reflect your current feeling state.

| Our team identified the best possible solution to our problem. | Our team did not identify a good solution to our problem. |

I___6 ___5 ___4 ___3 ___2 ___1 ___I

| Our team appropriately solved our problem. | Our team did not appropriately solve our problem. |

I___6 ___5 ___4 ___3 ___2 ___1 ___I

| Each person on the team was appreciated and listened to. | Not all people on the team were appreciated or listened to. |

I___6 ___5 ___4 ___3 ___2 ___1 ___I

| Communication was supportive and open. | Communication was closed and unsupportive. |

I___6 ___5 ___4 ___3 ___2 ___1 ___I

| Our team addressed process issues as well as content issues. | Our team only addressed issues related to content. |

I___6 ___5 ___4 ___3 ___2 ___1 ___I

Once you have completed the above statements individually, spend some time as a team discussing them.

Appendix D

Tips and Techniques for Building a Team

To a large extent, the success of your problem-solving efforts will be tied to your ability to mold your group into a TEAM—a group of people who are committed to solving the problem, who bring a high level of energy to the process, who are able to work well with others, and who are focused on quality (that is, process, customer satisfaction, continuous improvement). Well-functioning teams require effort—everyone must assume ownership of the product and of the interpersonal dynamics that occur within the group.

All teams can expect to move through a common cycle of growth and maturation. Different dynamics will surface at different points in the life cycle of the team. The process is successful when team members understand the normal cycle that all groups progress through. It is easier to deal with problems when you understand that your experiences are not unusual.

The stages that you can expect your team to move through (primarily based on the work of Tuckman):

    Form. This is the coming together stage. Team members are polite to each other as they get to know one another and get some sense of the team's assignment. It is typical during this period for members to be less personal and more watchful of each other. There is gradual growth in personal exchange as members seek to determine their place within the group. Personality and approaches to teamness emerge—some people are eager to meet and work with new team members, some hold back or are even hostile to the idea of group action, some will focus solely on the task to be addressed (content), while others will focus on the people in the group (process).

Storm. This is the political stage and is characterized by infighting, arguing, and withdrawal. Team members are sorting out personal relationships and vying for team positions and responsibilities (issues of power and influence). This is the period when interpersonal skills are most critical—how do we deal with our differences and learn to appreciate what each person brings to the table.

This tends to be a stage of low morale and productivity. All teams move through this stage; the difference between successful and unsuccessful groups is that the successful teams move on to the next stages, while the unsuccessful ones put all their energy into deciding who is controlling the group and thus stay bogged down in interpersonal conflicts.

Norm. This is the focusing on work stage and is the natural outgrowth for teams that have resolved issues around control. The team has moved through its interpersonal differences and is now able to focus its energy on the job at hand. The work is the critical focus of the team. Less energy is spent on conflict and members have decided they want to make the team work. At this point members are shifting their efforts toward mutual support and interest, but real caring for each other is not as important as commitment to seeing that the team goal is accomplished. This is a period in which productivity begins to increase.

Perform. This is the optimal stage. Team members understand the work to be done, they are comfortable with their interpersonal relationships, and they care enough about doing a superb job that they extend that caring to focusing also on the needs of individual team members. Team members are comfortable with each other, so informality among members is typical—there is a rapport and closeness among members. Words such as *loyalty, trust, affirmation,* and *belonging* typify the team atmosphere. This is a period when productivity is very high.

> **Because the team develops such closeness, there is the danger that the group can become insular in its attitudes and dealing with others (we have each other and don't need anyone else). The group can also be perceived as being arrogant (we are really good—better than anyone else).**
>
> **Such attitudes will make it very difficult for team members to move to other teams—they make comparisons between groups (and find the new groups lacking) and those on the new teams resent the individuals comparing the new group to the old.**

Mourn. This is the closure stage. A team has come together, achieved its goal, and is ready to end its cycle. There is a need to recognize that ending is a part of the cycle, and the group needs to plan for some sort of closure activity to acknowledge the ending (including the normal feeling of loss and separation; check some of the Kubler-Ross material on the psychological cycle associated with loss). If the team has functioned well, this should be a time for celebration.

WHEN YOU ARE FORMING A NEW TEAM

Plan to spend some time getting to know each other. Many new teams feel an urgency about the task and want to get to work immediately. However, the time spent in building relationships early in the team life cycle will improve dynamics later. Some things you can do to help the forming process:

- Plan get-acquainted periods. These can range from all members answering some basic questions about themselves (either directly or through partner interviews) to facilitated sessions using an instrument such as the Myers-Briggs Type indicator that allows members to get a sense of what characterizes and motivates each person within the team.
- Allow time for talking with a purpose of revealing or sharing feelings or establishing an atmosphere of sociability rather than of communication. This can be in the form of warm-ups (structured or unstructured) that start each team meeting. It might also mean taking a few minutes to chat

about any gossip that was heard since the last meeting—
sometimes the grapevine messages about what is happening
around the team's problem are appropriate.

- Spend time talking about the team life cycle—the forming,
storming, norming, performing, mourning stages—that
every team can expect to go through. When teams
understand up front what they can normally expect as they
develop, there is less disharmony as the group moves
through various phases.

- Allow time for playfulness—laughter is important and
reduces stress when things are tough. It fosters creativity
when the team is moving in new directions. Examples that
others have used: A name for the team, A plan that includes
playfulness. Recognition that is humorous.

REFOCUSING AN INTACT ONGOING GROUP

Teams sometimes get off to a good start and then lose momentum
during the problem-solving process. The process checks and evaluations that your team does at the end of each session can be a good
way of keeping on top of group attitudes. Whenever you sense that
the group is losing enthusiasm or direction, consider the following:

- Spend time going through new team-forming processes—
this is especially useful if you are a team that immediately
focused on the work to be done and did not allow time for
individuals to get to know each other. When a team needs
to retrace its team cycling, it generally requires a skilled
facilitator to help the group through the process.

- Dedicate a session to goal setting. This will allow the team
to refocus on the problem they are dealing with. Be sure
that the group identifies things like critical success factors,
goal or problem statement in 25 words or less, action plans
that have been detailed to include who will be responsible
and by when.

- Require agendas for all sessions and use your team's
guidelines—establish some structure for your team
interactions.

- Perhaps the group needs to reestablish the importance of
their activities—is the problem still critical? (Sometimes if

the process is extended over a long period of time, the group or the organizational need changes and the problem is no longer important enough for the team to spend time on. Or, the problem may still be critical and the group has simply lost sight of its mission.)

- Design in playfulness as a "required" part of group activity.

ROADBLOCKS THAT IMPEDE GROUP PROCESS

Even well-functioning teams will periodically run into group dynamics issues that make progress difficult. It is important to understand that impasses can be expected whenever people work together on matters in which they all have a vested interest.

Trap:	Having as a goal the elimination of *all* disagreement.
Solution:	Conflict, if it is focused on issues not people, is healthy. Team members can be expected to have different views. Arguing and discussing an issue is a healthy way of airing all sides and getting different viewpoints onto the table. The key is to remember the phrase, *Nothing personal*, as people talk through the issue.

Knowing some of the typical roadblocks can help the team recognize them as they occur. This can depersonalize differences among members and thus make it easier to deal with them. Common roadblocks that can be expected and some ideas on how to deal with them are:

Personality differences. We all approach the world differently. Quite often the things that others do that we feel are purposeful (done to irritate) simply reflect different approaches to a situation. If you find that some team members seem to be out-of-sync with others, you might consider having some sort of team-building activity that focuses on behavioral preferences. Using instruments such as the Strength Deployment Inventory, FIRO-B, or Myers-Briggs can help to profile each team member's way of approaching work and can help the team identify behavior patterns. Once they are identified, the group can develop strategies for optimizing differences so that members are more tolerant of each other and the team product is richer because all aspects of a problem are covered by different team member views-of-the-world.

Unequal contributions. For a team to have unity, it is important that each member carry his or her weight. If you find that some members are not, be sure team members fill out the forms provided for various steps in the problem-solving model. One of the advantages of writing out each member's responsibilities is that you have a visual picture of contribution. It is easy to ask a general question around everyone's name being equally on a matrix. The group can question why some members are not included or conversely why some have an excessive number of tasks and responsibilities assigned to them. The form depersonalizes the conversation and allows the topic of equal contribution to be addressed without anyone feeling he or she is being unjustly singled out. Be sure you account for breadth of assignments—don't just number count.

Can't get agreement. Some techniques that you might try:

- Taking a time-out when the team is unable to reach agreement. This means breaking for a while and then returning to the subject at an agreed-on point in time. This break can simply mean moving on to other topics or it can be a physical break.
- Break a larger topic that you can't agree on into subgroups. The team can focus on and get agreement on the smaller segments one at a time rather than dealing with the big composite topic.
- Have group members prioritize the elements of the topic under discussion. Once each person knows what is most important to him or her, the group can look for commonality especially among key driving elements. You

may agree on the things that are important and simply be arguing over the fluff elements.

No sense of belonging. This is something the team as a whole must agree to address. Some factors that can drive such feelings:

- The way in which the team was pulled together (no team building was done initially).
- The fact that team members may have very different working-relationship needs—some want to work in teams, others want to work alone.
- Management is giving the team mixed messages—work as a team; our organization rewards people for their individual contributions.
- Past history among team members—how they regard each other's skill sets.

Generally, this type of issue needs the help of a skilled facilitator.

Hidden agendas. To deal with these agendas, the team must be willing to put them on the table—this requires high levels of trust and mutual respect. Regularly scheduled meetings that require the attendance of all team members and which discuss even sensitive issues, can help uncover the hidden agendas. If the cause of this behavior is newness (team members haven't worked together long enough to know and respect each other), it will resolve itself as the team works together for a while. Otherwise, it will probably be necessary to have a skilled facilitator help the group to build trust and respect. This issue cannot be ignored if the team is to successfully resolve the core issue.

Difficult team members. Some people are simply more difficult to get along with than others. If you sense that a teammate falls into this category, the first step is to get a reality check. Observe the relationships that other team members have with this person— is it the same as yours, or are you the only one having difficulty with the person?

Sometimes we have difficulty with a person that no one else finds to be troublesome because of something within us. If this is the situation, spend some time looking at yourself. Ask yourself, "What is the hot button in me that this person is able to push? Why do I always react?" You can get help from a close team member or seek outside help from an interested nonwork party who knows you and can help you figure out why you are reacting.

If you discover through observation that everyone is having trouble with the same team member, you will need to decide what the troublesome behavior trait is and what you (at minimum) and the team (optimally) wish to do about it. There are some very good self-help books that define and explain difficult-to-deal-with behavior patterns and provide strategies for dealing with them. *Coping with Difficult People* (Bramson, 1981) is an excellent starting point. If the team member is critical to the success of the group (i.e., someone who cannot be removed or replaced), then you might consider getting help from an outside resource person who is trained in helping individuals or teams address their behavior styles.

If your team is faced with a personality issue, it must be resolved. Without resolution, you will stay at the second stage of team development—storming. Your product will lack quality and team members will become disillusioned with the team process.

Appendix E

Preparing Your Presentation—Tips

A key to effective presentations is to allow adequate time for preparation—good presentations don't just happen. You need to think about who your audience will be and then tailor the presentation to those who will hear it. This means that if you have several groups who will hear the message, you might need more than one version of the presentation. Plan some time for dry runs—decide who will be doing and saying what, and then get the room you will actually be using, if possible, and go through the actual presentation.

Some tips to help you during the preparation process:

Wear the hat of the audience. What do they want and need to hear about? Don't focus on your needs at this point because your effectiveness is determined by how well you meet the needs of those you are marketing to—not on how well your solution meets your team needs. Some questions to ask about your audience:

- What is the size of the group?
- Who are they—background information about the people attending (think in terms of why they are attending the session, their knowledge of the subject, what role they fill in the company, personal style—likes/dislikes)?
- How do they react to things that are new—personally, culturally?
- What benefits (WIIFMs) are there for the audience—how can you best present to be sure these benefits are covered in the session?
- What is their mind set about the subject—will you have to change attitudes or views about the topic?

Answer each of these questions wearing the hat of the individuals in the audience. Empathize with them; think of what you would want to hear in their position. Keep these thoughts in mind as you develop your presentation.

Use visuals and handouts when possible.   People tend to retain more of what they interact with rather than what they simply hear and see. If you have handouts to match your visuals, people have a reminder to take with them and something to write their memory-jogging thoughts on during the session.

If you use visuals and handouts, they must be as perfect as you can make them. If you don't know all the rules for developing good materials, get help. Many organizations have a department to do this. If you have to do it on your own, read some good reference books that will talk you through the requirements for both visuals and handouts. Poorly prepared materials will do your case more harm than good.

Plan for the presentation.   The guide below can help you walk through the preparation process.

Objective of the project:	The why of the project stated in 25 words or less.
Objective of the presentation:	What is your intended result? Understand the difference between presentations (sharing information) and working sessions (focus on joint problem solving and idea generation). Each format requires different planning and will result in different outcomes.

Participants:
  who they are:
  what they will talk about:
  why they are included:
	List of presenters: ☐
	                                ☐
	                                ☐
	                                ☐
	
	List of attendees: ☐
	                              ☐
	                              ☐
	                              ☐
	                              ☐

Agenda: How will you structure the presentation—
                           develop an outline for the total session. Basically
                           you want to
                           ■   tell them what you will tell them,
                           ■   tell them,
                           ■   tell them what you told them.

Mechanics: ■   Plan for time and location. Make any
                               necessary reservations. Most people don't
                               like presentation sessions that are longer
                               than one and one-half hours. Working
                               sessions, however, can be longer—often a
                               day or more.
                           ■   Decide whether to provide food; if you
                               plan to, make the necessary arrangements.
                           ■   Be sure that agendas and any other pre-
                               session materials are mailed in sufficient
                               time for attendees to get and review.
                           ■   Determine what equipment will be needed
                               (flip charts, overhead projector, etc.)—
                               arrange for it and allow time for testing on
                               the day of the presentation to be sure it all
                               works.
                           ■   Are supplies needed? (Handouts, writing
                               supplies, etc.)

Meeting room: Select a space where you will not be interrupted
                           and where individuals will feel comfortable.
                           Check the environment—room arrangement,
                           temperature, outside noise, etc. Remember to
                           reserve extra time so that you can PRACTICE.

Elements That Need to Be Considered in Developing *a Presentation*

Use the following template as a guide for developing your presentation.

Note:	Some people use index cards to get their thoughts about their presentation onto paper. An advantage of the card method is that you can easily arrange/rearrange ideas and make changes to one element at a time.

GUIDELINES FOR DEVELOPING A PRESENTATION

Step 1. Write out the purpose for your presentation—to inform, to persuade, to move to action. You will need to develop a concise statement that explains exactly what you are presenting. It is a statement that should stand on its own—no additional information is needed for people to understand what the presentation will be about.

Step 2. Develop an opening statement—something vital and attention getting. You will hook your audience with this statement, so be sure you know them well enough to know what they will listen to. Openings can be humorous, fear focused, factual, outlandish—any of these work with the correct audience. Keep in mind the purpose of your opening—get your audience listening to what you are going to say because they see a value to them in the presentation's content. Sometimes you need to do this step last after you have thought through the entire presentation.

Step 3. Develop supporting information—this is the heart of your presentation. Its purpose is to prove the value of your initial intent statement. Use whatever means are necessary to explain your ideas—visuals, statistics, stories, examples, figures (match the content and approach to the audience's style). Focus on developing bullet-type statements as proof. These are more likely to retain the attention of the audience.

Step 4. Develop your action-getting conclusion. Tell your audience what kind of action you want them to take and why it is to their benefit (remember WIIFM). Too many people don't ask for action at the conclusion and don't understand that their lack of a request is what caused the inaction.

Elements That Need to Be Considered in Making a Presentation

Above and beyond the mechanisms of the presentation, here are some points that you will need to remember when you are actually making your presentation:

- Know your audience and speak to them.
- Assume an attitude of customer service. How can I help them? What do they need to hear to buy into my presentation?
- Speak slowly and distinctly.
- Watch the nonverbal messages being given by the audience and respond to them.
- Use questioning whenever possible—listen to the customer, speak less.
- Stay positive and upbeat.
- Respect the customer—stay within time limits, give them processing time.
- Plan for summarization points—don't give too much information in one chunk, check to see that people have understood your message. Remember that the presentation process is as important as environment and presentation mechanics.

Elements of a Good Visual/Handout

Good visuals and handouts will enhance your presentation. The key is that the visual or handout you use must enhance the overall quality of the presentation. They must not detract from your content by transferring the audience's attention away from your message and onto the visual material itself. Some questions you might ask yourself in deciding whether to incorporate materials into your presentation:

- Will the visual/handout help you communicate your message more effectively? This might refer to completeness, impact or clarity.
- Will you be able to do a quality job with the material—will it be interesting, done perfectly?

- Will you be able to reference the material effectively during the presentation—you know it well, reference points are logical and flow easily with the presentation?
- Will the material help your audience better understand the content, or, will it potentially distract?

If you plan to use any visual aids, be sure they are concise (no more than 30 words per overhead maximum). Remember KISS (keep it short and simple). When done well, visual aids add to the presentation; otherwise, they detract. Dont' forget technology—there are some excellent graphics and presentation packages available that can make your material very professional (even to the point of animation and audio).

Tips for Using Flip-Charts

- Best with smaller groups—25 maximum (everyone must be able to easily read the material that is written onto the chart).
- Use colored markers, intersperse color for effect but no more than three or four colors per page.
- Check mechanics—easel is secure, flip-chart is attached securely to easel.
- Use water-soluble markers for writing and have masking tape handy to mount completed pages.
- Leave a blank page at the beginning of your presentation—when not using the chart, flip to a blank page (avoids the chart becoming a distracter).
- Turn to your audience when you talk—this may mean you can't write and talk simultaneously (a reason to use a scribe).

Tips for Preparing Transparencies

- Limit content—no more than six to eight lines of text (each item should contain no more than eight to ten words) written in phrase format.
- Use color, boldface type, and large type.
- Use bullets for listings.

- Select a simple typeface.
- Use frames to avoid white space around the transparency sheet.

Tips for Using Transparencies

- Know the machine you are using—check it out beforehand.
- Cut the light whenever you are not using the overhead—a sheet that flips down to cover the light works better than turning the machine off and on.
- Face your audience when talking.
- Use a pen/pencil to reference points on the transparency itself, use a pointer when referencing the screen.
- Don't block the view of your audience.

Finally the key to a successful presentation can be summed up in three words:

PRACTICE!   PRACTICE!   PRACTICE!

Learning Transference Worksheet

> **This worksheet is to be used after you complete your initial problem-solving initiative. Then refer to the worksheet periodically to make sure that you continue to grow in your problem-solving skills.**

List the team-problem-solver skills that you'll be bringing to your daily work environment:

_____

_____

_____

_____

_____

Identify three work opportunities for applying the seven-step problem-solving process.

_____

_____

_____

Who can help you in addressing these areas? What specifically do you need from each person?

_____

_____

_____

_____

What problem-solving tools do you want to standardize in your workplace?

_____

_____

_____

What will you have to do to ensure that they become part of your work environment?

_____

_____

_____

_____

_____

List three things that you learned about yourself by going through a team-based problem-solving experience.

_____

_____

_____

How will you use this knowledge to ensure that you are an effective
TEAM PROBLEM SOLVER?

_____

_____

_____

_____

_____

Bibliography

Articles

Brown, Darrel. "Ch-Ch-Change!?" *Management World* 15, no. 8 (Nov.-Dec. 1986), 24–25.

Kanter, R. M. "Change: Where to Begin." *Harvard Business Review*, July-August, 1991.

Post, Frank G. M. "Beware of Your Stakeholders." *Journal of Management Development*, 8, no. 1 (1989), 28–35.

Tuckman, Bruce. "Developmental Sequence in Small Groups." *Psychological Bulletin* 63 (1965), 384–99.

Books

Ailes, Roger. *You Are the Message: Secrets of the Master Communicators.* Homewood, IL: Dow Jones-Irwin, 1988.

Albrecht, Karl and Ron Zemke. *Service America: Doing Business in the New Economy.* Homewood, IL: Dow Jones-Irwin, 1985.

Berry, Dick. *Managing Service for Results.* Research Triangle Park, NC: Instrument Society of America, 1985.

Bone, Diane, and Griggs, Rick. *Quality at Work: A Personal Guide to Professional Standards.* Los Altos, CA: Crisp Publications, Inc., 1989.

Bramson, Robert M. *Coping with Difficult People.* New York: Dell Publishing, 1981.

Braddard, Michael, ed. *The Memory Jogger: A Pocket Guide of Problem Solving Tools.* 2nd ed. Methuen, MA: Goal/QPC, 1988.

Brassard, Michael. *The Memory Jogger Plus+.* Methuen, MA: Goal/QPC, 1989.

de Bono, Edward. *Lateral Thinking: Creativity Step by Step.* New York: Harper Colophon Books, Harper and Row, 1973.

de Bono, Edward. *Six Thinking Hats.* Boston: Little, Brown and Company, 1985.

Desatnick, Robert L. *Managing to Keep the Customer: How to Achieve and Maintain Superior Customer Service throughout the Organization.* San Francisco: Jossey-Bass Publishers, 1987.

Crosby, Philip B. *Quality is Free.* New York: Mc-Graw Hill, 1979.

Fisher, B. Aubrey. *Small Group Decision Making: Communication and the Group Process.* New York: McGraw-Hill, 1974.

Fisher, R., and W. Ury. *Getting to Yes: Negotiating Agreement without Giving In.* New York: Penguin Group, 1983.

Heron, John. *The Facilitators' Handbook.* London: Kogan Page, 1989.

Juran, Joseph M. *Juran's Quality Control Handbook.* 4th Ed. New York: McGraw-Hill, 1988.

Lele, Milind M. with Jagdish N. Sheth. *The Customer is Key: Gaining an Unbeatable Advantage through Customer Satisfaction.* New York: John Wiley & Sons, Inc., 1987.

Martin, William B. *Quality Customer Service.* 2nd Ed. Los Altos, CA: Crisp Publications, Inc., 1989.

Orsburn, Jack D., Linda Moran, Ed Musselwhite, and John H. Zenger. *Self Directed Work Teams: The New American Challenge.* Homewood, IL: Business One, Irwin, 1990.

Partnering for Total Quality, Vol. 6—A Total Quality Tool Kit, *SEMATECH*, 1990.

Peters, Tom, and Nancy Austin. *A Passion for Excellence.* New York: Random House, 1985.

Schotes, Peter. *The Team Handbook: How to Use Teams to Improve Quality.* 4th Printing. Madison, WI: Joiner Associates, Inc., 1989.

Senge, Peter. *The Fifth Discipline.* New York: Bantam Doubleday Dell Publishing Group, 1990.

3M Meeting Management Team. How to Run Better Business Meetings. New York: McGraw-Hill, 1987.

vonOech, Roger. *A Whack on the Side of the Head: How to Unlock Your Mind for Innovation.* New York: Warner Books, 1983.

Walton, Mary. *The Deming Management Method.* New York: Putnam Publishing Group, 1986.

Other Resources

Barker, Joel. *Discovering the Future: The Business of Paradigms.* Order video from: Charthouse Learning Corporation, 221 River Ridge Circle, Burnsville, MN 55337, Phone: (800)328-3789.

Malcom Baldrige National Quality Award Criteria
National Institute of Standards
Route 270 and Quince Orchard Rd.
Administration Building, Room A537
Gaithersburg, MD 20899
Phone: (301)975-2036

Index

INSTRUCTIONS FOR ACCESSING
THE FORMS FILE

The enclosed disk contains a file with blank copies of all the forms included in *The Team-Based Problem Solver.* These forms can be copied exactly, or you can copy a form to a new document and then alter it to fit your particular needs.

For **DOS-based** *Machines*

The file is a Microsoft Word for Windows file. To access the file:

1. Run the Word for Windows program (Version 2.0 or higher is required).
2. Perform the FILE OPEN command.
3. Change to Drive A.
4. Select the file named **FORMS.**
5. Click on the OK button.

For **MAC** *systems*

Requirements to access the file:

- A machine that has a SuperDrive or FDHD drive.
- Microsoft Word Version 5.0 or higher.
  Apple File Exchange or similar IBM-MAC translation program

To access the file:

1. Open the file translator.
2. Put the disk in the drive.
3. Click on **FORMS.DOC.**
4. Click on Translate.
5. Open the Microsoft Word program.
6. Open the file called **FORMS.DOC.**